They tell me that 80% of all Christian books are read by women. I predict that this trend is about to be wonderfully 'bucked' by this book. While believing its message will snatch from destructive fire, it will also powerfully start another cleansing one.

The late Derick Bingham
Adjunct Professor of English Literature at
John Brown University

Disarming honesty, alarming reality, personal experiences and biblical bombshells all combine to make this book fascinating reading. In the midst of love and laughter, suffering and pain, bereavement and romance, a life story unfolds. Fire fighting as a job, and sin fighting as a life commitment, are just two of the strands in Mitch's journey. This personal story of vulnerable humanity and amazing grace will inspire and instruct. Seeing God at work, in the life of someone I can identify with, has stimulated in me a hunger for God himself. Any book which does that is well worth reading. Prepare to be stirred to pray, aroused to action, and motivated to be real with God. This book will start some fires of faith which no firefighter on earth will extinguish!

A great read, but, more importantly, it bites where many of us need to be bitten!

The Right Reverend Ken Clarke
Bishop of Kilmore, Elphin and Ardagh

This book grabs your attention from the first sentence and will hold you through to the end. It is funny, well written and aimed to change lives. Buy it and then give it to a friend.

R. T. Kendall
author and speaker

Engaging and eloquent, this book is a story of real life written by an ordinary man, but it is also the story of sin and the need for grace. Mitch has beautifully articulated that the answers to the needs of this broken world can be found only in Jesus Christ.

Gavin Peacock
former Chelsea FC and
Queens Park Rangers Captain

For firefighter Mitch there is nothing more rewarding than a successful life-saving attempt. He himself has been rescued and lives to tell others how they too can be saved for ever through Jesus Christ. Mitch is one of my heroes of the faith. You'll grasp his heart for God as you read Snatched from the Fire.

John White
President and Chaplain to Firefighters
For Christ International

Snatched from the Fire

Mitch

Foreword by J.John

Snatched from the Fire

Life with a purpose

ivp

INTER-VARSITY PRESS
Norton Street, Nottingham NG7 3HR, England
Email: ivp@ivpbooks.com
Website: www.ivpbooks.com

First published 2011

British Library Cataloguing in Publication Data
A catalogue record for this book is available from the British Library.

ISBN: 978–1–84474–502–9

Typeset in Great Britain by CRB Associates, Potterhanworth,
Lincolnshire
Printed and bound in Great Britain by Ashford Colour Press Ltd,
Gosport, Hampshire

*Inter-Varsity Press publishes Christian books that are true to the Bible
and that communicate the gospel, develop discipleship and strengthen
the church for its mission in the world.*

*Inter-Varsity Press is closely linked with the Universities and Colleges
Christian Fellowship, a student movement connecting Christian Unions
in universities and colleges throughout Great Britain, and a member
movement of the International Fellowship of Evangelical Students.
Website: www.uccf.org.uk*

Dedicated to the memory of
Gerald Titmus
and
Derick Bingham

Contents

Acknowledgments

My thanks to Pauline, Steph, Faithe and Michael for proof-checking my text. Also, thanks to Green Watch, Knock, my home church, Orangefield Presbyterian, and Revd Ken McBride.

Thanks to all the staff and directors at Crown Jesus Ministries who supported me on this adventure, especially Pip – working with such a great team is a dream. Thanks to my wife, Amanda, and our children, Noah and Megan, for your love and patience – I adore you. Finally, thanks to my very special friend, Jesus. You can make me laugh and cry like no-one else, and I am in awe of your sublime perfection. I love how you tell a story, make time for the needy and inspire the weak, and how you died on a tree for me.

Foreword

I am delighted to recommend this book to you for three reasons.

First of all, Mitch is quite simply a good friend and fellow evangelist whose work I value: from my experience, anything he says is worth listening to.

Secondly, in this book Mitch interweaves Christian teaching and real life in a way that is both compelling and utterly biblical. It is not uncommon to hear speakers and preachers whose teaching, for all its merits, seems to be separated from reality. The result is a message that can sadly seem inauthentic or even irrelevant. The pattern in the Bible is of theory and practice shown together. We read not just of Moses' teaching, but of Moses the man; we are not just told what Jesus taught, but we are shown Jesus himself. Even with Paul, that greatest of theologians, we see interspersed with his teachings accounts of a flesh-and-blood man wrestling with applying the message of the gospel to his own life. That invaluable pattern of God's Word and a human life interwoven is here in this book. In these pages you will read of a real gospel and a real life. Learn from both!

Finally and most importantly, this is in every sense a *good* read. It is a common rule of Christian books that the deep ones are dull and the entertaining ones shallow. *Snatched from the Fire* breaks that glum rule. It is at the same time entertaining and educational, compelling and challenging, interesting and instructive.

Read this book, be blessed by it and pass it on to someone else for them to be blessed too. Thank you, Mitch. You have put us in your debt.

J.John

Introduction:
Why read this book?

He lives with his son in a clean little semi-detached house with simple furniture and net curtains. He moves slowly, even shuffles a little, and his brown shoes are always shining, just like his face. When he speaks he is a master at pausing mid-sentence, processing his words carefully as his hands move with elegance to the tones of his voice. Leaning towards you when communicating truth, Charlie always has something worth saying. Sharp as a knife and bright as a button. At 102 years of age he loves to tell his story, or should I say, God's story.

One day at his house he leaned on me and said, 'Listen Mitch, we must never get away from the message of Jesus – we need to focus on this message again.'

This book is a response to those words. This is not a book about religion, nor is it a book that has all the answers. It's my story and my musings mixed up with God's wisdom from the Bible. It is my attempt to help people understand the greatest message ever told. Read it; laugh, cry, smile and allow Jesus to come close.

Mitch
July 2010

1. Dracula:
The problem is me

The blood was catching the back of my throat as I slowly began to regain some sense of consciousness. I felt nauseous from the smell and taste of blood as I held a cotton rag to my mouth, catching the watery mess running off my lip. I looked a sorry state but I didn't care. I just needed to get to a safe place and recover. Given a couple of hours, I would be strong and ready for action again.

The drugs were beginning to ease off, but not fast enough to allow my legs to function. Walking was a challenge, and any change of direction was almost impossible. Like a drunk on a bouncy castle I wobbled and struggled. Failing to negotiate a left-hand turn on the corridor, I almost went to ground. In fact, had I not received some assistance, I would have been flat on my face nursing another wound.

Finally we were outside, and I slumped against the wall while my accomplice waited anxiously for our car. Things were not going to plan. Our rendezvous point was overcrowded, the pick-up was running late again and I was going nowhere fast. It was windy, grey, cold and threatening to rain. Belfast was always threatening something, especially at that time in our history.

At last a red Cavalier pulled up in front. A quick glance at the registration plate confirmed it was our man. DXI 9164. We made our way over, faces screwed up in the wind and rain. I was bundled into the back seat. In the front there was the usual silly argument: 'You were late, Gerry.' 'No, you were in the wrong place!' I was silent with the exception of the occasional whimper. I was a victim – at least that's how I felt.

A visit to the dentist is a horrible thing. At least it was for me at the tender age of ten. If my introduction seems like something from an Andy McNab novel then there is good reason for it. My experience of the dentist was one of capture, interrogation and torture. Mum was always the supporting act, while Dad when possible supplied the getaway vehicle. The short walk to the dentist was fine for Mum and me, but while I was coming off the ether (or whatever else they filled my tiny lungs with), I would never manage to climb the hill home. The getaway vehicle was essential.

For all his smiles, my dentist intimidated me. He looked like Dracula – not that I have ever seen Dracula – but the Count from *Sesame Street* and snooker legend Ray Reardon gave me an idea of his appearance. His surgery was on the first floor, but if you needed a tooth extracted you stayed downstairs. After you passed the reception window you entered the waiting room, which was not exactly an explosion on your senses. Once-white net curtains hid a grey outside wall, and hanging on the magnolia walls they had a faded picture of a child. She was dressed in Victorian rags, clutching the arm of a teddy bear and leaning pitifully against a stone wall – perhaps she had visited my dentist too. The furniture was a mixture of plastic chairs and chrome-framed seats with brown padding. In fact, the furniture at our hut in the local dump was better! The waiting was as bad as the extraction – the butterflies in my stomach would eventually leave to be replaced with a thousand flapping seagulls.

Finally, after what seemed like an hour of prayer and fasting, the dentist would escort me into the torture chamber. The room was clinical in appearance, with a large black leather-like chair holding centre stage. Once in the chair there was no return. My dentist would smile (I never trust a man in a white coat who smiles, except of course Mr Ruddock, my woodwork teacher) and place a black rubber mask over my mouth and nose while turning on the gas. I would try to resist, tears running down my cheeks. I would give my mum a look that yelled a million silent cries for help.

What were my parents thinking of? I was terrified. Even now I can smell the rubber mask and hear the sound of the gas. Let's make no bones about it, the extraction of that tooth at the hands of my dentist was one of the most traumatic moments of my life. He asked me to count to ten slowly, and I felt the seat spinning off into the darkness and a whirring noise developing in my head before I passed out.

Someone asked me recently if I had been afraid of the dentist as a child. I said 'no'. Fear was too inadequate a word! Petrified, panic-stricken and scared to death would be much more apt. No offence to my dentist or my parents, but what were they thinking? I will never put my kids through that . . . Do dentists still use gas? I don't know. I don't plan to find out either.

* * *

Anyway, welcome to my book. The fact that you have got this far is a great encouragement to me. I'm not the most educated bloke, so it's quite an achievement to write a book, let alone have someone spend money on it and actually take the time to read it. This is a book about me. It's also a book about God. These are the two most important personalities in my life, and most of the time I come first – that may not seem like the right thing to say but it's the honest one – and this is an honest book.

That dentist visit sticks in my mind for another reason. Some weeks afterwards I got on the number 32 bus with my mum and headed for the city centre. Mum was unusually quiet (if you ever met my mum you would know how unusual this was). Something was brewing . . . 'Keith (how I hate that name), if I ask you a question will you tell me the truth?'

Now that is never a good question to ask – especially a mother to her child. I had three options:

1. Say yes and lie.
2. Say yes, tell the truth and upset her.
3. Say no and upset her for ever!

I went for option one. It's amazing how you can justify a lie sometimes, but I seriously didn't want to upset Mum.

'Yes, Mummy, of course,' I replied in my very best Oliver Twist impersonation.

There was a pause as she composed herself before asking, 'Do you say bad words?'

How did she find out? What did she expect me to say: 'Yes, Mum, of course I do; all the big footballers say bad words. Would you like to hear some?' That line would have been wasted. By the age of ten I had picked up quite a few new words that I hadn't learned at home. Listening on the sidelines at football games and in the company of older boys in our furnished-better-than-the-dentist's hut, I had developed a colourful vocabulary – many of the words for which I still needed a definition.

'No,' I replied, with a face that changed colour and revealed I should have said 'yes'.

Mum began to unfold the story of what had happened at the dentist's. After Dracula had extracted my tooth and I had slowly begun to recover from the effects of the gas, my dark side had got the better of me. I had hurled abuse towards the dentist which would have been better placed in Al Pacino's *Scarface*. I had kicked the nurse and thrown a full bowl of my blood all over her. And all this in front of my mum. Possibly no more than they deserved, some might say.

Now you may laugh, but on that number 32 bus I wanted the red plastic seats to open up and swallow me. I picked at the chewing gum under the seat as Mum finished off the story, now explaining how very upset she was with her boy. She didn't go into every detail, but it was clear that my choice of words, being both varied and colourful, left little to the imagination.

How was I to get out of this one? I felt like a budgie with a broken wing cornered by a hungry cat. What if Mum told Dad? 'Just wait until your father gets home' was a phrase used frequently in our house, as Dad was the voice and hand of authority. Then I would be a budgie cornered by a lion. I shifted in my cigarette-scorched seat trying to find an excuse: 'I don't know, Mum, but I don't say bad words – honest!'

Mum was very disappointed. I felt sick – sick with guilt, sick with worry, sick with embarrassment. There was no point in digging a deeper hole for myself, so I sat quietly. I had been found out and I blamed Dracula!

Who taught me to do wrong? To lie, cheat, steal, curse and throw a tantrum? No-one ever sat me down and trained me to be bad. But put me in our hut with a couple of mates and it just came naturally. Of course I was influenced by others: Stephen showed me how to raid the apple trees, Gary showed me how to steal from the milkman's van (just wait until he is on the fifth floor of the flats), Darren showed me where to get magic mushrooms and Colin showed me how to make a fake ID, but no-one trained me to be bad in the first place. I seemed to sway naturally towards doing wrong and being downright selfish.

My childhood was very happy. It was bathed in good people teaching me good things. My parents, older brothers, neighbours, schoolteachers and relatives all had a genuine desire to see me grow up to be a 'good boy', and in the eyes of most I probably was.

However, I also had a dark side that seemed to assert itself all too often. At the dentist's I cursed, kicked, lied and blamed someone else for my failings. 'Harmless,' you may say, but ask the nurse how she felt when she received the kick and had her whites covered in the contents of the bowl (my slobbers and blood!), not to mention the volley of foul language that spewed out from the angry face of this vicious little ten-year-old boy.

The truth is, from the moment you and I were born we were more than capable of doing wrong.

'Who stole the cream bun from the tray?' a mum asks the three-year-old boy standing in front of her.

'It wasn't me,' he replies, as he wipes his hands on his once-clean dungarees, the cream and jam smeared over his lips and nose.

It may be a cute picture but it reveals our true human nature. No-one taught the kid to steal the bun; he just wanted it. He knew he shouldn't, but the desire for the bun was greater than the law that stopped him. We will lie, steal and cheat in order to get what we want. The biggest motivation for doing wrong is me, me, me, me and me. It is true that the environment we are brought up in influences us, but even if you and I had lived in the most perfect place on earth – some sort of Garden of Eden – we would have followed Eve and taken what was forbidden. (In fact, I think Eve was a better person than me – I wouldn't have shared it with Adam! Gollum-like, I would have hidden in the corner of the garden and declared, 'It's mineses!')

So was it the apple on the tree that caused the problem? No, it was the 'pear' on the ground! The brilliant C. S. Lewis (from my neighbourhood of East Belfast) once confessed, 'For the first time I examined myself and found what appalled me: a zoo of lusts, a bedlam of ambitions, a nursery of fears, a harem of fondled hatreds. My name was Legion.'[1]

The apostle Paul (not from East Belfast) declared, 'What a wretched man I am! Who will rescue me from this body of death?' (Romans 7:24).

I can relate to those feelings as I look over my life. Some people have skeletons in their closets; I have dinosaur fossils in aircraft hangers! My past is littered with moments of wrong and regret. I know that learning from your mistakes is part of growing up, but I seem to have made an awful lot of them. Sometimes the boxes in my mind pop open and shout in a Jack Nicholson voice, 'Remember me? We go back a long way . . . '

Truth is, I have hurt more people than I want to remember. Most of the time I try not to give my dark side a second thought. There is something wrong with me, something broken that needs fixing. I suspect you are like that too.

In our minds we all too often try to justify our wrongs. We ask the questions:

'What is right and wrong anyway?'

'Who decides these things?'

'Can there be any absolute truth?'

Let's find out . . .

2. Lemon and Peartree Hill: Broken world

Mrs Woods was small, but that didn't mean she was soft. She had a pleasant demeanour but you should never have mistaken her meekness for weakness. As maths teachers go she was pretty good, friendly but firm. My mate Arthur the gardener still sees her and happily cuts her grass in the summer months. Funny how she introduced him to accounts and now she is paying for it big time!

I didn't like maths. In fact I've lost count how many times I failed maths tests. My brain can only concentrate for short periods of time, and double periods of maths left me shattered and hungry. They should have advert breaks every ten minutes in class – adverts for toys and cereals (the ones with the cute girls in them) – and allow you time to grab a pack of jelly sweets from your school bag. Actually, I didn't like most subjects in school and I really hated English. In primary school I remember faking stomach pains for two weeks so I didn't have to read aloud in an English class. Only when the doctor suggested that my parents take me to hospital did the miracle in my small intestine begin. I was healed within an hour.

In secondary school I tried to avoid any project or class that required public reading, and when I went on to technical college it was just the same. I remember when we all had to give a report in front of a video camera about our recent work experience. I was sick with worry, skipped class and as a result never completed the module in career development.

So there I was sitting through another double period of maths trying to keep my head down, pretending I was invisible and probably thinking up an excuse to escape. In geography that same year Stephen and I had put Sellotape on my lips and ripped it off just to get them to bleed, giving me an excuse to visit the nurse. Stephen had pulled it so hard I thought I would need a skin graft! I would have jumped at an opportunity to leave maths, any excuse – except this one. The principal came to the door and called Mrs Woods over for a quiet chat. I could see them looking in my direction with serious expressions. I feared the worst. Had I been dropped from the school football team?

Jackie Gallagher, our principal, was football mad. It wasn't unusual for him to interrupt a lesson to come in and chat about last night's footy match or his latest coaching visit to China. The world's greatest-ever football player, George Best, had attended the school, and often football seemed a greater priority than academic achievements. My friend Gerald used to say, 'If you went to our school and had an O level, you were the principal!'

Maybe I hadn't been dropped from the team; perhaps I was in trouble and in for the cane! Mr Gallagher kept a cane in the glass corner cabinet, and any boy who stepped into his office for misbehaviour was reminded that it was there. In five years at the school I only ever recall one incident when he used the cane, and it was on me. I remember it cracked my hand so hard that my mother felt it. She was so disappointed.

Back to maths class, where Mrs Woods called my name and asked me to go outside and see the principal. In the corridor he put a hand on my shoulder and said that my brother was on his way to collect me. He didn't make eye contact and it was obvious that he didn't want me asking any questions, so I didn't.

My dad had gone into hospital just a few weeks previously to be treated for a condition called multiple myeloma, a cancer of the bone marrow. Dad was, as I remember him, brilliant. My immediate thoughts are of his infectious laugh. He had a big red-faced laugh with tears in his eyes. There was no action of my dad's that I didn't study as a work of wonder. I watched him shave – the foam and all too often blood mix being peeled off with perfect strokes from a single blade. I watched him drink Guinness, read the *Belfast Telegraph* and snore on the sofa with perfection. He was a brilliant machine of a man who enjoyed watching and playing football, golf, snooker, cricket and darts. He would sink a putt and celebrate like Seve Ballesteros by pumping his fist in the air; score a goal and raise his hands like Ricky Villa; hit the stumps and shout 'How's that?' It was not possible to love someone more than I loved my dad. He made time for me, called me his 'wee Johnny Miller' (a golfer with a similar hairstyle to mine at the time) and collected me from school for lunch one day a week. Saturday was our night in. My brothers would be attending youth clubs or discos, my mum out with her friends at the golf club, but Dad and I would stay in, watch *Match of the Day* and order a curry chip from the local Chinese takeaway.

Dad had a great circle of friends and over the summer we would often visit them and their families. I would listen as they told stories from their youth and watch as his big laugh and smile would light up a room. I remember one of his old Boys' Brigade friends telling me of how he and my dad broke into the local church just to play table tennis. The summer was also a great time for family holidays. We would pack up the car and travel to Morecambe, Bournemouth, Great Yarmouth, Skegness or Butlins in Ayr. I loved those holidays of lazy days on the beach and going to a show at night. By the time I was thirteen I had seen The Krankies, Jimmy Tarbuck, Lenny Henry, Michael Barrymore, Freddy Starr, Little and Large, Cannon and Ball and *Crackerjack* live. We stayed in guest houses or flats that had rooms painted magnolia and smelled of cigarette smoke and air freshener. Some nights we would sneak into big hotels for the free entertainment. On other nights we went to speedway, greyhound racing and my favourite, wrestling. The last year we went on holiday together Mum and Dad let me go to the wrestling on my own. It was brilliant. I met Stu Francis ('Oh I could crush a grape!') in the bar and Princess Paula bought me a coke. Wrestlers like Giant Haystacks, Big Daddy, Fit Finlay, Bomber Pat Roach and King Kendo Nagasaki were all stars, but none as brilliant as my dad.

But just before Christmas Dad had gone into hospital for the first time in his life with a recurring problem from an old football injury. One week later he had been diagnosed with multiple myeloma and now he was fighting for his life.

My brother picked me up from school in his lime-green goblin – an awful-looking Ford Fiesta. On arrival he told me that Dad wasn't doing well and we were going to visit him in hospital. He didn't want to talk about it and changed the subject abruptly. At the hospital we gathered together as a family and went in to see Dad. Because he had been in an isolation ward for four weeks, I had been peering in at him through a thick glass window and blowing him kisses. Now I was able to hold his hand, feel those big thumbs pressing my knuckles, kiss him and feel his stubble on my cheek. He smiled and spoke briefly with each of us; his face looked grey and tired. I just watched in silence as my brilliant machine of a dad began to break down. As we left, my brother Philip said to him, 'We'll see you later, Dad.' But we never did. At the time I didn't understand how serious things were but, looking back now, the way Mum held it together was a testimony to her toughness. We prayed with the minister in a side room. Outside the sky was the colour of steel but the heavens were made of brass.

I got home around 7 pm and Mum stayed at the hospital. The house was full of relatives and neighbours as news got through that Dad's condition had deteriorated. That night I prayed that my daddy wouldn't die. As I threw darts at the board in the kitchen, I struck a deal with God. If I hit the bullseye he would let my father live. I threw until my arm was sore – I never did hit the bullseye.

At 6 am my brother Colin woke me up, sobbing. That night my bullseye god had robbed me of the most special person in the world. 'Daddy's dead, Daddy's dead,' my brother sobbed, and tears flooded my world like never before. Mum gathered her little chicks around her and told us to be brave, but we could do nothing but weep – my world had been torn apart. I spent days just crying and cursing my bullseye god. By the time the funeral arrived I had no tears left and I was exhausted.

People say 'Time is a healer' and that may be true, but time never removes the scars of suffering. I bear a scar from that day and a river runs through it. Over twenty years later I cannot write about that moment without the paper becoming wet with my tears. Dad didn't suffer greatly when he died, but our family did, particularly Mum. With a husband of more than twenty years gone, she now had three teenagers to look after alone. In spite of our loss my teenage years were mostly happy times, but often in silence the tears, hurt, anger and frustration of not having my dad would rise like a volcano. Colin, my eldest brother, would often take the position of father figure, and Philip, my other brother, became an important role model. A committed Christian and talented footballer, he was always there when I needed him. He read the Bible with me, bought me reading notes and helped me use them. However, as brothers do we would sometimes argue and fight. I can remember how mid-argument Philip would often shout at me, 'You've got a chip on your shoulder, son', and I would rage in anger, but he was right. I *did* have a chip on my shoulder. I wanted to tell him I missed Dad and wanted him back. I missed his laugh and the feeling of his stubble. I had missed the bullseye, so maybe it was my fault.

* * *

Fast-forward ten years and I am on a mission trip to Kenya.

When I was invited to preach at a local village crusade, the Kenyan experience was full of pleasantness for this young white man who preached about Jesus. I drove past the mud-hut village and stayed in a nice house with a security guard on the gates. I ate good food and even had a maid on hand should I need anything. However, by the second week my good friend Rev. Samuel Muriguh decided he did not want me to leave Kenya without experiencing the 'real Africa'.

We took a bus to Mathare Valley, Nairobi's largest slum area, occupied by over 180,000 people. The experience changed me. I walked beside open sewers running through the muddy tracks between shanty huts. Chickens pecked at garbage stacked beside corrugated walls, goats showed their ribcages as they lay tied to poles, and children began to gather around the white man in the valley. Today I can still smell Mathare Valley. One child came close and held my hand. She was about six or seven years old and had green snot on her lip with flies stuck to it. I didn't know if I should wipe the snot or swat the flies away, so I let go of her hand and did neither. She looked at my once-white Nike trainers and then back up at me. I felt sick as she climbed into my head and snuggled against my brain.

The poverty and neglect were overwhelming. It was four years since I had traded my 'bullseye god' for the God who whispered forgiveness on a cross, but I wondered where he was in that little child's world. Did he not care about this little girl, her family and her future? There was a workshop run by the Presbyterian Church which was doing a fantastic job giving people life skills in needlework, pottery and suchlike. Their work was valuable but it didn't solve my dilemma. Surely God could do more than this? I bought two clay cups and saucers as well as some placemats as my way of supporting their work and easing my guilt, but the little girl still sleeps on my brain.

* * *

It's 2004 and I am on a trip to Romania.

We arrived in Budapest and crossed the Hungarian border, travelling a further four hours to the town of Oradea. After three days of digging a trench to provide water for a new school, I decided to take the opportunity of visiting children in the local hospital. To be honest, looking back, my motivation was probably just to get my bald head and aching muscles out of the sun for the day!

On arrival at the hospital and after spending a brief spell with the toddlers, I was instructed to go to the third floor and spend an hour with a baby wearing a lemon Babygro. I remember being quite nervous as I climbed the stairs: what would I do with a baby? I didn't even know how to hold one! She was lying behind the white metal bars of her cot on a plastic-coated mattress; she was thin and quiet. An American volunteer with a local charity explained the circumstances: the baby had been found in a rubbish skip; she had no toys, no clothes and no name; she was approximately ten weeks old and malnourished. Under Romanian law she could not be adopted for two years and would spend most of the time in her cot with limited mental stimulation and a few feeds and nappy changes per day. Human contact was predominantly down to volunteers from local foundations and charities. Like many babies who arrived there, after two years she would develop mental problems and no-one would want to adopt her.

I picked Lemon up (I didn't know what else to call her) and held her in my arms, praying and weeping. I felt so helpless. It was one of the most profound spiritual experiences in my life, and Jesus was in me as I ministered to Lemon, and Jesus was in Lemon as she ministered to me. For an hour I held her, played with her, sang nursery rhymes, fed her and changed my first nappy. I wept again that night in my room in Romania. I wanted to bring her home, protect her and love her. Where was God in this broken, messed-up world? I could blame the Romanian government, I could blame communism and its appalling effect through the dictatorship of Nicolae Ceauşescu, but could God not step in and rescue Lemon? At least give her a name?

* * *

Back in Belfast now and it's 15 December 2000. I am riding a fire engine as team leader at Green Watch, Knock. Neither my fifteen years' experience nor any amount of training could have prepared me for what happened next. It was a frosty morning and we were out on the appliance doing the usual morning messages at the start of a four-day shift. Davy Booth was in charge when we got a call through on the radio: 'A061, A061, turn out, turn out to a road traffic accident at Peartree Hill, Comber Road, over.'

We were mobile and planning our strategy en route. Putting on our fire kit and hi-visibility jackets, we were aware that we would be first in attendance and would probably arrive before the paramedics. Paul would grab the hose reels, Brian would get the cones and cutting tools, while I would join Davy in assessing the casualties. Harvey was driving and he took the last corner with caution knowing that the accident was probably just ahead. He was right.

A car had collided with a lorry and inside the car were two teenage boys. As Davy and I approached the car the full scale of the carnage became apparent: both boys had died on impact and there was nothing that could have been done to save them. Sometimes people exaggerate when using descriptive words but this was in every sense horrific. It was our job to clean up the mess from the accident, lift the lorry, remove the bodies and clean up the fuel and any other fluids. It was a sombre afternoon as the crew worked together for over four hours alongside other emergency personnel. These were someone's children with so much potential. Why hadn't God taken the frost off that section of the road? Could he not have allowed the lorry to be thirty seconds late before travelling down the road?

Why did God allow this to happen? Paul asked me that very question on our return to the station. He asked about my faith and how I would cope with the day's events. The truth is that I didn't really have a good answer. I struggled to find the right words, but what might have sounded right somehow lacked substance. A year later 'Ken the Counsellor' from the fire brigade called in to see how the crew were coping. Since that incident we had encountered a few nasty road accidents and it was his job to 'follow things up'. Ken told us that we have little compartments in our minds like a chest of drawers and sometimes after a traumatic incident those drawers won't stay closed. They keep popping open – even when we don't expect it. Peartree Hill had this effect on me, and not only on me but on the others who attended the accident.

* * *

Why does a God of love allow so much suffering? Dad and Mathare Valley, Lemon and Peartree Hill – they all seem to stack up like a deck of cards. I could tell of witnessing a man being beaten to a pulp outside a pub, of a man smashing a bottle over his own brother's head, of cruel lies leaving a child in tears, of threats that drove another to suicide. Why?

And there is of course a much bigger picture.

Why did 800,000 people die in the war in Rwanda in 1994, leaving 350,000 orphans?[1]

Why were 800,000 Ukrainian children affected by the Chernobyl disaster?[2]

Why on 26 December 2004 did a tsunami with the force of 1,000 atomic bombs kill over 220,000 people?[3]

Why do nearly 11 million children each year not live to see their fifth birthday due to a lethal combination of malnutrition and mostly preventable diseases – a catastrophe that experts say is needless?[4]

The truth is that the suffering in your stories, my stories and indeed the whole world's stories points to something deeper. If the first chapter highlights that I am broken and need fixing, then this chapter highlights the fact that I am not alone: the whole world is messed up and broken. We live in a broken world with broken people, and suffering seems to be one of the ways this brokenness expresses itself.

Now what follows may disappoint you, but I am not going to attempt to answer your questions on suffering. To do so would make me arrogant, ignorant and narrow-minded. This book may be held by crippled hands, resting upon legs in a wheelchair or sitting in front of a cancer patient. I don't know your situation and I don't have all the answers to the suffering in this world. If Mother Teresa and Billy Graham couldn't answer that question, what qualifies me to do so?

Suffering can often be a mystery that we do not understand, and it is hard to make sense of it especially when we watch others go through it. But at other times it is obvious that man's inhumanity to man has played a key role. In one of his memorable statements during the Second World War, Winston Churchill said that 'the heart of the human problem is the problem with the human heart'.[5]

Have I broken the speed limit recently? Have I read a text message while driving or behaved carelessly in some other way? What hardship could I have caused? Is it fair to blame

God for my carelessness? In truth, until you and I are doing everything possible to eradicate suffering and pain in the world, what qualifies us to accuse God?

An article in *The Times* once asked, 'What's wrong with the world?' In all the correspondence that followed, the shortest letter was by far the best:

> In response to your question, 'What's wrong with the world?' –
> I am.
> Yours faithfully,
> G. K. Chesterton

Our own greed and selfishness often leave us suffering as a consequence. However, suffering should not lead us to conclude that there is no God, but rather to ask, 'Where is God? What is he like? Why does he allow suffering to happen? How does he respond?' Of the hundreds of Christians I have met who have endured suffering at some level, I personally don't know of one person who has rejected God as a result. However, I know many that have found God *in the midst* of their suffering. Perhaps God will at times use suffering to get our attention for a greater purpose. C. S. Lewis wrote, 'God whispers to us in our pleasures, speaks in our conscience, but shouts in our pains: it is his megaphone to rouse a deaf world.'[6]

While my late friend Derick Bingham was going through his third course of chemotherapy, he shared with me over a coffee that in the midst of the trials and pain Jesus had provided him with 'inexpressible, undiluted, unadulterated joy!' Weeks later as news broke of his death I was reminded that God wastes nothing – every scrap of suffering, every failure and all the pain he will use to shape me and others.

If you and I are often part of the problem, can we also be part of the solution?

And if so, can I fix myself or do I need help?

When I was a kid I would often push my BMX bike towards my dad with a flat tyre, broken chain or bent crank and ask, 'Daddy, can you fix it?' I asked not because I was lazy but because I didn't know how to fix it myself.

If there is a God, maybe we should ask the same question of him, rather than just point an accusing finger.

'Daddy, can you fix it?'

His answer might surprise us!

3. Sex:
Who decides what's right and wrong?

Now there is a nice little title to keep you reading a bit longer! To all those who have skipped chapters 1 and 2 just to get to what you hope will be the 'juicy bit', shame on you! I once read in a magazine that men typically think about sex once every ten minutes. If that is the case then my title is right on cue for many of you. But how did they gather the data for that statistic anyway? How did they possibly measure it? Did they just stop blokes in the street and ask them what they were thinking about? How do you measure a man's thoughts? And is that statistic the average over a lifetime or just for the teenage years? If that statistic is true, then as a teenager I was not the average, for every ten seconds would have been closer to the truth!

The brilliant Adrian Mole wrote in his diary *The Cappuccino Years* of how he awoke at 3 am in his London flat with a desire for Opal Fruits. Having no packets in his flat he went outside to try to buy some. In the first two minutes he was offered sex, drugs and a fake Rolex watch, but it took thirty minutes to find an innocent packet of Opal Fruits. What does that tell you about the world we live in? That story could have two effects on you: (1) it makes you aware that our 'freedom-of-choice-twenty-first-century culture' has gone too far, or (2) it makes you want to go and live in London!

I was twenty years old when I met my wife, Amanda, and she was hopelessly beautiful: my flower, my Audrey Hepburn, the single star in my night sky. Alexander Smith wrote, 'A man gazing on the stars is proverbially at the mercy of the puddles on the road',[1] but there has never been a puddle that has been any more than a minor inconvenience in the last sixteen years.

At the time I met Amanda I was working as a fitness instructor and leisure attendant and she was a pupil at a local girls' school. Each week her class came in to use the leisure facilities and we would catch each other's eye. She was seventeen and stunning. She attended my home church on Sunday mornings as well as the youth fellowship and Girls' Brigade. Through a mutual friend we began to chat and eventually I plucked up the courage to ask her out for a date. It was approaching Valentine's Day and one night over a coffee and a chat with my brothers and their wives I suggested it was time to make my move. They laughed as I declared in *Wayne's World* fashion, 'She will be mine, oh yes, she will be mine.'

Sunday morning came and I checked the balcony to see if 'Audrey Hepburn' was in attendance or having breakfast at Tiffany's. I couldn't see her and spent the entire service worrying how else I could make contact with her before Valentine's Day. To my relief, after the service there she was standing outside chatting to friends. I waited at a distance for my time to move like a lion in the long grass. She turned and headed for the gate alone – I pounced!

'Hey, Amanda,' I said in my coolest-possible East Belfast accent without sounding like I had been possessed by a Californian (why do people put on American accents to sound cool?).

'I was wondering if you would fancy joining me for dinner on Valentine's night?'

Two days later we laughed and ate in Gigolo's Italian Restaurant in Belfast before exchanging a kiss outside the Pizza Pie Factory. She smiled the sweetest smile of innocence and turned her face into the bow of my neck as I held her. The world fell into the shadows as time stood still. If it had not been for the insistence of her parents that she be home by 10 pm I think I would still be there, frozen to death in the winter chill.

A few months later I planned for us to have a night in with a movie at my house. I dimmed the lights and we cuddled up on the sofa with snacks and drinks to 'watch' the latest film out on video – not a good idea, young people! Mum was next door and seemed to pop her head into the room every fifteen minutes with some pathetic excuse. My mum didn't trust me with girls; *I* didn't trust me – I was like a dog in heat, a wild hungry animal, and even with all the Christian virtue in the world to help me, my hormones were still going crazy. You cannot possibly cuddle up to your girlfriend with the lights dimmed and not be sexually turned on! It's a good job I had a strong woman. We had set out the ground rules early in our relationship, and with much prayer and self-control we had the victory. My good friend Derick Bingham had been leading a series on sexual purity and helped me put a strong foundation in place. The rules were simple:

1. What's covered, keep it covered!
2. Nights together are best in the company of friends and family.
3. A couple who pray together stay together. Keep short accounts with each other and with God.

That night before she left for home, I held Amanda in my arms as soft background music set the scene. With my heart beating in my throat and my head on her shoulder I said, 'I love you.' Now you may laugh or feel like you are going to vomit but I thought I did love her! She was soft, tanned and gorgeous, but I had miscalculated. As I spoke those words with the lights dimmed and Lionel Richie singing 'Dancing on the Ceiling' (kids, don't try that at home either!) in the background, I waited for a reply . . . and I waited.

She said nothing. She didn't even say I like you! The next twenty minutes or so were unbearably awkward until her mother picked her up to go home. I was furious, furious that I had been so stupid! I wanted her to be like putty in my hands, but things had not gone to plan. I was now in a position of weakness; my desire to 'own' her had backfired and now I felt like I had played my 'ace' too soon.

As I lay in my bed that night I tried to make sense of her reaction. Albert Einstein once wrote: 'Some men spend a lifetime in an attempt to comprehend the complexities of women. Others preoccupy themselves with simpler tasks such as understanding the theory of relativity.'[2] Women are very complicated; they are wired differently from men. Everything in their head is connected to something else. The word 'love' to a young woman means many things. It speaks of lifelong commitment, sharing, family, trust, safety, honesty and perhaps sex. To a young man it means sex with a level of commitment. I wanted to blame her for my pain, but the truth was that I was a self-seeking little rat! I thought of other girls I had dated, other girls I had whispered those words to, and then I realized I had no idea what love was. I knew what sex and romance were but that's a far cry from love. I thought about the selfishness that navigated my own existence and my morals and how they were driven by me. Maybe I should be locked up in a straitjacket?

Amanda and I dated for four years before we got engaged, and another two years after that we finally tied the knot on a windy day in October. I stood at the front of the church a bag of nerves, and as Michael began to play Handel's *Messiah* I looked over my left shoulder: she looked like an angel – my flower was in bloom. I look back and count it a great blessing that over those years we held our ground on moral purity and she could wear white on her wedding day, not so much with pride but as a testimony to the goodness of God. Of course she eventually did say 'I love you' but not before time, only when we both understood the true meaning and power of those words. Love is a wonderful thing and I don't know if you can understand love until you first understand something of the love of God.

* * *

Living as broken people in a broken world we have a broken view of sex. Hunger, thirst and sex are three of the most fundamental urges we have. The first two keep us alive and the third makes sure we continue to exist. The problem with sex is, it's so very good and so very dangerous! I can't think of anything else that, for Amanda and me, one moment was completely wrong and the next moment (after our marriage vows) was completely right (although not in front of the wedding guests!). I struggle with sexual urges like any bloke. The moment I became a Christian, and indeed the moment I got married, my sexual temptation was not cured. We are all among other things sexual sinners.

I remember ten years ago walking into one of the bedrooms at Springfield fire station in Belfast and discovering a pornographic magazine on one of the beds. I was off the fire engines that night as we had enough men on duty and they were all out at a fire call. I stood frozen in the bedroom, the battle raging between the temptation to pore over its pages on the one hand and the desire to follow the will of God on the other. I began to walk towards the magazine. It was like a magnet pulling me in. Then I stopped and rocked to and fro on my heels, clenched my fists and shook my head. Had anyone seen me they would have called for the men in white coats. Eventually I fled the room.

Not every time has there been such a victory, but I have built into my life some very strong defence mechanisms (see chapter 10, p. 129, on church fellowship). My view of pornography is simple: if you are prepared to ogle the nakedness of someone else's daughter and someone else's wife for your own temporary gratification, then you must be willing to let others do the same with your wife and daughter. One of the scariest prayers I ever prayed was 'Lord, if I look, may I be found out.'

Sex is a good subject when talking about right and wrong. What is right and what is wrong can become complicated. Who sets our moral code on sex? Over the past twenty years the laws that govern sexual behaviour have shifted significantly. I am not referring so much to the law of our government but to our own moral law. What is allowed on television, magazines and computers today and what we see as acceptable to wear in public would have been seen as totally unacceptable even fifteen years ago. Sadly, sex is too often a taboo subject in many churches, especially when you consider that it is the most talked-about and most visually promoted subject in our world today. You may applaud our postmodern society with its liberal views on sex, but the consequences are seen everywhere: AIDS and other sexually transmitted diseases and infections, teenage pregnancy, careless abortions, human trafficking, child pornography, rape and prostitution – none of which any right-thinking person can celebrate. There is an obvious danger that we are heading for a lawless society with regard to sex. Freedom of choice is saying, 'I make my own laws when it comes to sex', but that is a dangerous path. You can believe that you are sincerely right in your choices but so too did Adolf Hitler! Sincerity on its own is not enough.

What is right and wrong? If you had to place a Yes (for right) or a No (for wrong) against the following list of ten I wonder how you would fare:

- Pornography
- Sex education for seven-year-olds
- Under-age sex
- Casual dating

- Sex before marriage
- Co-habiting (my mum used to call it 'living in sin')
- Adultery
- Multiple partners
- Homosexual practice
- Bisexuality

From my survey among non-Christian men, seven out of the above ten questions were answered with a 'yes' of approval. (You would have received quite different results just twenty years ago.) A survey also shows that seven out of ten people fall into the category of being 'relativists'.[3] This has nothing to do with their aunt or uncle but refers to their views on life in general. These views in essence say: what is true for you does not necessarily need to be true for me; what is right for you does not have to be right for me. It's all relative . . . Relativism is a fascinating religion believed by people who are religious about not being religious. Our society is multi-cultural, multi-religious and as a result multi-choice. It's loose. People can pic 'n' mix, cut and paste like some religious version of the song 'Mambo No. 5'. We are influenced by what we see and today seems to be all about choices and consumerism. We declare there is no absolute truth, no absolute right and wrong, for there is no right- and wrong-giver! We are evolving social animals who have no fixed point of reference. The trouble is, when I set my own boundaries I can always find an excuse to move them.

I read a story in a newspaper of a bloke who was sent a speeding ticket through the post by his local council. He decided to appeal and go to court, convinced that he was not speeding on that particular stretch of road, as his little 50cc motorbike was not capable of travelling at the suggested speed. Weeks later in court they discovered that the camera had miscalculated. It worked on a system that takes a fixed point of reference such as a brick wall or the road and then calculates the speed of the moving vehicle against this reference. However, in this particular case the camera used a bus moving in the opposite direction as its 'fixed reference' and therefore miscalculated!

In many ways today's society moves fast and free, resulting in three consequences. First we have no fixed reference of right and wrong; secondly we are reluctant to think clearly about our views as this may force us to change direction and admit we are wrong; and thirdly we are particularly reluctant to take seriously anyone who makes absolute claims – especially Jesus! However, we need absolutes in life – otherwise our world becomes nonsensical. Either the pages of this book are paper or they are not. You cannot say, 'Well, they are paper for you but they are metal to me!' Of course lots of things are a little grey, but too many people living in the grey will lead to disaster. Either casual sex is wrong or it's right, but it cannot be both.

* * *

Going back to pre-Amanda days, at seventeen I was young and free. Life was a gentle breeze of good friends, girls, alcohol and on occasions recreational drugs. A group of twelve students from my college set off on a three-week trip to Denmark. We travelled in a yellow school bus with bench seats and a restrictor fitted so we could travel no faster than fifty-five miles per hour. Our journey took us through the Republic of Ireland, Wales, England, Holland, Germany and finally on to Denmark. I don't think there was one day when we were not drinking alcohol. We stopped for two nights in Amsterdam and I was as free as a bird and soon as high as a kite, and Darren and I wasted no time in setting off on foot to find the infamous red-light district. I remember after about a twenty-minute walk turning the corner and seeing a beautiful young Filipino woman standing in a shop window wearing very little. She smiled and waved for us to come in for a fee of what was about £25 at the time. The street was full of opportunities for sex, but while other guys went to shows and took advantage of what was on offer, Darren and I declined. After thirty minutes in the red-light district we felt sorry for those girls. We wanted to buy their freedom and release them. There was a law working in us which said that this was wrong, that sex was not to be cheap and dirty. Here were two teenagers in the land of sexual opportunity and all we wanted to do was buy the girls their freedom. On the way back to the apartment we bought a Mars-bar-sized block of blow and smoked our heads off. The next day we visited the beer factory and I shared with Darren how I wanted to free those girls like Elliott had freed the frogs in *E.T.*

* * *

There was a law of right and wrong working in me in Amsterdam and I am glad I obeyed it. Now I hope we can agree that there is a law of right and wrong working in our lives. But who determines what this law is, and are we mature and honest enough to recognize that we are all very good at breaking this law at times?

Ask yourself these questions. How has your behaviour been today? Have you behaved as you would expect others to behave? Have you fallen from your own standards, never mind anyone else's? In Belfast we have a phrase that I like: 'Go and take a good look at yourself!' Now we don't like people highlighting that we are breaking the law, so I am sure you are already finding excuses in your mind, perhaps even some pretty good ones, to put this book down, but the reality is this: we need laws in our world and the fact that we break them should not be our excuse to ignore them. People everywhere have an innate sense that they ought to behave in a certain way and cannot really get rid of it. They know there are unspoken rules and yet they still break them. The apostle Paul in the New Testament writes, 'I do not do the good things I want to do, but I do the bad things I do not want to do' (Romans 7:19, New Century Version). To understand this is the foundation of all clear thinking about ourselves. You and I cannot just choose to live by our own code, setting our own standards, making our own rules to suit our weaknesses and vices, for to do so would cause anarchy.

Also, the law of right and wrong must be something above and beyond us. We need a right-and wrong-giver or we will for ever find excuses to avoid the punishment we deserve for breaking the law. We will justify our actions to avoid the punishment. 'If you do the crime you do the time' is a saying I am sure you have heard of. We have often seen people on our TV screens who have committed crimes, and because of some stupid loophole in the law they got away with it! How does that make you feel? I know I cry, 'Where is the justice in that?' This is the law working through me, and if I expect it to be working in others too then I am not exempt.

And it is our duty to know the law. When I visit France on holiday, I endeavour to find out their rules for driving and obey them (even if I do think they drive on a silly side of the road). If you drive your car at forty mph in a thirty mph area you cannot stand before the judge and say, 'Your Honour, I didn't see the sign for thirty mph, therefore it is not my fault; I should not be punished because I didn't know!' To suggest such a thing before a judge will earn this stern reply: 'Ignorance is no defence in a court of law.'

Christianity is much more than a list of do's and don'ts. It is not a moral rod to break our backs, forcing us to live a life of guilt. It contains the law of God and it reminds us that we all break this law, but it also shows us how we can be set free.

Christianity is deeply liberating as it offers forgiveness based not on ignorance but on the fact that someone else, Jesus, has taken the punishment you and I deserve. The Bible tells us that the law is written upon our hearts, and that this law like any other brings judgment to those who break it. Until we first recognize that we are guilty of breaking God's law, Christianity doesn't make sense.

Now God's laws are also known as the Ten Commandments. You may know a few of them but let me paraphrase them for you:

Do not have other gods before me; do not make images and worship them; do not take my name in vain; have a rest day and keep it special for me; honour your parents; do not murder; do not commit adultery; do not steal; do not lie; do not desire and lust after your neighbour's possessions.

These commandments act as a mirror to show us how broken and messy we are. We have all lied, stolen something and even committed adultery, for Jesus said, 'Anyone that looks at a woman lustfully has already committed adultery with her in his heart' (Matthew 5:28). The law convinces us of our guilt and because of this we either attempt to cover our sins or we never look in the mirror. The Bible also says that if we break one of God's laws we break them all. Now if you stand before God the righteous Judge, what will his verdict be: innocent or guilty? How does that make you feel? Let's not bury our heads in the sand and avoid the issue. Remember, 'Ignorance is no defence in a court of law!'

You may try to defend your case by saying that you have also done a lot of good and charitable work in your life, but this does not excuse you from the verdict! Imagine that you are guilty of speeding, and standing before a judge you tell him that this morning you made your wife breakfast in bed, yesterday you gave £1,000 to a local charity and tomorrow you will be teaching children about the dangers of recreational drug use. Will he excuse you for speeding? Of course not!

We cannot live up to our own standards never mind God's, and our own good deeds do not change the verdict. C. S. Lewis said this:

> Christianity tells people to repent and promises forgiveness. It therefore has nothing (as far as I know) to say to people who do not know they have done anything to repent of and who do not feel they need any forgiveness. It is after you have realised that there is a real Moral Law, and a power behind the law, and that you have broken that law and put yourself in the wrong with that Power – it is after all of this, and not a moment sooner, that Christianity begins to talk. When you know you are sick, you will listen to the doctor. When you have realised that your position is nearly desperate you will begin to understand what the Christians are talking about.[4]

You and I and everyone else in this broken world need help. We cannot fix ourselves. The explorer Sir Ranulph Fiennes recently climbed to the top of Mount Everest at the age of sixty-five. Reporting from the summit he said, 'This is the closest you can get to the moon by walking.' As I listened to his report from the comfort of my living room, I couldn't help but think, 'For all his huffing and puffing he is really no closer to the moon than I am sitting at home!' To attempt to repair our sinful nature is like an apprentice plumber who stands before Niagara Falls and says, 'I think I can fix this!'

I happen to believe that religion is not the solution either – Jesus is! Religion is all about man trying to reach God and claim that he is on their side. Christianity is about God trying to reach man so that we can be on his side. Christianity is the belief that Jesus the Son of God gave up the riches of heaven, wrapped himself in skin, was born in a stinking animal shed, died a horrendous bloody death on a cross, and all so that we might be fixed. This is the story of Jesus and I want to introduce him to you. He is a personal friend of mine. But before I do that let's look at one other important issue: the church.

4. A box of chocolates: Loving church

I have in some shape or form belonged to church all my life. As a child, church was similar to my old grandmother. Although very nice, she was grossly out of fashion, a bit slow, short-sighted and I didn't like her kisses. When I visited her on Sundays she would make cold rice pudding with prunes for dessert. I would feel sick at the sight if it! She would give Dad a Rich Tea biscuit and stewed tea in a china cup, the handle of which he couldn't get his fingers through. She would bring out an old biscuit tin filled with chipped toys that harboured enough germs to wipe out a hospital ward. Following a goodbye kiss at the door you got a boiled sweet. That was Granny's house – and that was church for me – nice, but please don't make me go there too often.

On Sunday mornings I would lie in bed afraid to move, hoping that my parents would sleep on and we would miss church. There used to be an advertisement on TV that asked, 'Can you put a fruit pastille in your mouth without chewing it?' I found the answer: only in church! Sucking fruit pastilles, counting bald heads, drawing on the hymn books and anything else I could possibly do to help pass the time. Church was torture; surely I should not have to sit through this while the sun was beaming in the sky? My early memories of church are that it was always sunny outside. We sat next to high windows that let in as much daylight as possible as they whispered tauntingly during the service, 'Look what you're missing, kids!' They have since covered the windows, removed the clock and added coloured lights. Now it's more like a Las Vegas casino, though without the cocktails and slot machines!

On arrival I would have my little card stamped to register my attendance and be given a small sweet. The more times you attended over the year the bigger the book/prize you received at the end of the year at a special service. The system was called 'The League of Church Loyalty'. I don't know what message it was supposed to send out to little children, but looking back I think that the idea is seriously flawed. It implies that God rewards more highly the kids whose parents have cars and can come to church when it's raining. It says that God has a league and we need to compete and work in order to please him. While the sermon was on 'grace [undeserved favour] alone through faith', it seemed to us that merit was by attendance alone! The system was full of legalism and I often wondered if they used those details for any other purposes . . . (I am suspicious by nature!) On Award Sunday there was always especially loud applause from the church congregation for the boy who came the most weeks, but for the child who came only five Sundays there was a distant clap from a few family members who were then left feeling embarrassed for not being 'proper church members'. It was Noah's Ark pop-up books for the top attendees and jotter-paged colouring books with pictures of Joseph in a grey coat for the rest. As for the top attendee, his dad was an elder and had to be seen in church every Sunday with the family. His dad was a clever man with a big car; maybe they should have given the pop-up book to his dad? And if my memory serves me right, that boy disliked church just as much as I did, so how was that fair?

Some Sundays my parents would sleep in, but on most occasions my dad would rise early, walk to the shops for the Sunday newspaper, wash the car and make a big pot of porridge for the family. That porridge was like wallpaper paste. I can remember him making me eat it, and gagging because it was so thick and sticky. One morning my mum reminded me that there were starving children in the world who would be glad of it. I scooped the contents of my bowl into an envelope and told her to post it to them. She called for my dad, but before he came downstairs to give me a good smack I had eaten the porridge and assured him my comments were only an innocent joke!

By the time I ran into my teenage years Granny was dead, and so too was the church. Well, at least it felt that way on Sunday mornings. Now church was like a middle-aged school-teacher suffering from an identity crisis: moody, caring, angry and loving all mixed together in the pot. This teacher had my best interests at heart but was too busy to spend time listening to or understanding me. Church was mostly warm and friendly but sometimes it felt cold and intimidating. I was challenged about my lifestyle but sometimes I misunderstood this as a threat.

At the summer church youth mission the preacher warned me that one of two things could happen: I could leave the building and get run over by a bus, or Jesus could come back and find me drinking beer in the park. I'm surprised I didn't develop a phobia of buses and parks! I enjoyed the Boys' Brigade, a fantastic organization, on Friday evenings. Youth club on Saturday nights was a brilliant place to chat and meet up with friends, but I hated the idea of being forced to stop playing football to listen to someone who I felt didn't want to do a talk in the first place. Let me explain: each week a different leader had to do a ten-minute 'churchy bit' called the epilogue. (What a strange and untrendy name to give a talk you don't want to go to in the first place.) You could spot the leaders who had prepared and those who had not. You could also sense their unease as many of them struggled to grab our attention. I had the perfect solution: leave me with the football in the hall, and if the leader wants to connect with me, he can do nets. Eventually I was banned from the youth club. A bearded bloke came to see me and Stephen at the Boys' Brigade to tell us we were not allowed back. The previous week Stephen and I had masterminded a brilliant escape plan just before the epilogue in order to go to the local Chinese takeaway. As the bearded leader expressed his disappointment, Stephen choked on his coke and spat it all over the floor. We were in kinks of laughter and the leader was obviously upset by our lack of remorse. Three months later I left the Boys' Brigade too. I was fifteen and life had simply too much to offer. Church was becoming like detention in school and I didn't want a teacher as a friend.

Years later Forrest Gump reminded the world that 'life is like a box of chocolates; you just don't know what you might get!' Church back then was a box of chocolates and all too often I was left with the coffee truffle, and for a teenager that's just not cool. Over the next four years my general attendance at church or any of its activities was sporadic, and with the exception of Christmas, Easter and before exams, which were important occasions on my church calendar, church was off-limits.

In the eighties Northern Ireland was quite different from the rest of the UK for obvious reasons. Countless idiots were bombing the place to bits in a pathetic and painful attempt to win a war that all too often seemed a little pointless to me. It's not as if we have a hundred billion barrels of oil underneath us or we're rich in gold! We do have sheep, potatoes, the Giant's Causeway and a shipyard, but it's hardly the Emirates! During 'the Troubles' church was important for many families because it helped to define us. People wanted to know if we were a 'Protestant' or a 'Catholic', and so if our name didn't give this away people would ask what church or Boys' Brigade we belonged to. Being a Protestant family, belonging to Orangefield Presbyterian Church was an important part of our identity.

Church has an important role in Christianity and I want to focus on it for that reason. Ask people the first words that come into their minds when they think of Christianity and they will often list 'church' in their top three. People automatically associate church with Christianity, and rightly so. However, church has sadly become the most unattractive, misunderstood and disappointing aspect of the Christian faith. People often have negative experiences and can even be angry with the church. Some understand it to be an out-of-date, grumpy law enforcement officer who shouts 'Hell' to anything enjoyable. For others church is a social club for the elderly and vulnerable: for others it is manipulative, greedy and self-seeking; and for others still, it is boring, irrational, irrelevant and a massive killjoy which is full of hypocrites. Television presenter Noel Edmonds said, 'The church is the dullest experience that we have in this country.'[1]

According to a recent survey, if all the people who fell asleep in church were placed in a row, end to end . . . they would be a lot more comfortable! Church can be incredibly boring unless you are plugged into the message. We are not used to sitting in one place listening to a lecture for over thirty minutes, and our attention span always struggles on a Sunday morning, especially as Saturday evening tends to be the main social night and often a late one too.

For an outsider looking in, many churches can be a kind of sub-cultural ghetto. People dress differently; their vocabulary is different; they sing songs about being 'washed in the blood' often to tunes dating back more than 150 years. If you walk in with your jeans on, newspaper under your arm, and park your pit bull terrier at the front door, many church members would have a heart attack! Rap group Naughty by Nature once said in their lyrics, 'If you ain't never been to the ghetto, don't ever come to the ghetto, 'cause you wouldn't understand the ghetto.'[2] Sadly there are times when we could replace the word 'ghetto' with 'church'. Television doesn't exactly make the church very marketable either! Stephen Gaukroger writes:

> Television portrays clergymen as fanatical bigots, wet, effeminate wimps who wouldn't harm a fly, or simple idiots. Church congregations seem to consist mainly of elderly women who meet in ancient buildings and participate in some obscure ritual that appears to involve little more than entering a building, singing a few old hymns and being asked to part with hard-earned money to help prevent the steeple falling down. A club with three rules – turn up, sing up and cough up![3]

I was nineteen when I became a Christian (more about that in chapter 9) and my first experiences of church were quite strange. Through the invitation of a friend I visited a Pentecostal church. It was an evening service and they had drums, piano and acoustic guitar playing traditional tunes, while some ladies in the front row waved and tapped tambourines with red, white and blue ribbons on them. The drummer had long hair and looked like he belonged to a rock group but had been ordered to drop the fancy stuff and keep a simple bass, snare and closed high-hat beat. Some people waved their hands; others it seemed were singing their own song with a different tune and I just stood and watched, feeling very much like the odd one out. The pastor soon came to the stage: grey hair, grey suit, grey face (grey was definitely in vogue) and carrying a red accordion. It looked like one of those trendy black and white photos where the centrepiece is in colour, only the accordion in the picture wasn't trendy. He belted out a few of his favourites and the tambourine crew went wild, some ladies slipping off their heels to do the 'Pentecostal two-step'. He preached for what seemed like an eternity, and although I couldn't under-stand all that he was saying he was definitely preaching with passion. I wasn't a Christian and although everything was very surreal and weird there was a strong sense of belonging, family atmosphere and love. I was made to feel very welcome.

A few months later I visited a different Pentecostal church about two miles away. I discovered that this was a church split from the previous church and that many of the members no longer spoke to one another. Eventually I settled in my parents' home church and, although it was lacking in all the energy of a Pentecostal church, I found the ingredients there that make me very proud to call Orangefield Presbyterian Church my home.

Church is full of flaws and because it is the main witness to the community people see the flaws first, highlighting them before they even consider its strengths. Someone once said to me, 'Mitch, if you find the perfect church, don't join it – you will ruin it!' That was good advice for we are all flawed, and so when we get together, no matter how much we try to cover them up, the cracks are still there. We also need to remember that many people who attend church are not Christians, and their lifestyle may not be a fair picture of all the God colours that can be seen within the church.

I once read a story of how the evangelist Billy Graham was being criticized and one person who said, 'Billy, you will put the church back a hundred years by doing this.' Billy responded, 'I did want to set religion back, not just 100 years but 1,900 years, to the book of Acts!'[4] That's exactly what church needs to do: get back to the basics of what God intended it to be when it was launched 2,000 years ago.

So what is church really?

When the Bible refers to 'church' it is not referring to a building, a meeting or an old-fashioned institution; it's simply referring to a group of Christians. Church is a collective noun like a herd of cows or a pride of lions. The harmony group Acappella Vocal Band (AVB) once sang these words:

> You can't go to church as some people say,
> It's common terminology we use every day.
> You can go to a building you can sit on a pew,
> But you can't go to church 'cos the church is you.[5]

Church is a group of Christians who do life together, and if you think about it it's quite a large enterprise. My good friend J.John tells this story:

> I find it difficult to know what to say when people ask me, 'What do you do?' If I say I am a canon in the Church of England that doesn't mean anything to most people so I have started being a little bit creative as I explain to people what I do.
>
> I met a woman in Heathrow Airport and we chatted briefly about our travels before she asked, 'What do you do?'
>
> 'Well,' I said, 'I work for a global enterprise, and we have outlets in almost every country in the world. We run orphanages, homeless shelters, hospices, hospitals, we work in reconciliation, justice work and basically we look after people from birth to death and we deal in the area of behavioural alteration.'
>
> She said 'Wow!' really loud so that everyone turned around. 'What's it called?' she asked.
>
> 'It's called the church; have you heard of it?' I said.

The church for all its faults does an amazing amount of good work and it's a pity that people only seem to focus on the negatives. In our world today there are incredible needs and I can think of no better organization to help. Half the world (around 3 billion people) cannot read or write. They live on less than £1.50 per day and cannot get a glass of clean water.

Around 1.1 million children die each year of malaria; 10 million little girls are in child prostitution because their fathers need the money to buy bread for the rest of the family; 14 million children are orphaned because of preventable diseases.[6] These are not just statistics, for behind them are real people with real stories, and I believe there is only one organization in the world large enough truly to make a difference and it's called the church.

The global church is a massive organization which is broken up into many denominations following all kinds of models. According to David Barrett's forty-year study in the *World Christian Encyclopaedia* there are 33,820 denominations in the world today. A more recent study has actually put the figure at 39,338! The reason for so many denominations is very simple: people are tribal; we like to have leaders and meet in groups, each group hoping to have one up on the other.

Maybe it's because I'm from Celtic roots, but I welcome denominations and all the diversity within the church. Indeed, I believe this diversity is wonderful. I have the privilege of speaking in many different denominations and I enjoy the diversity of styles and God's rainbow of people each responding to their convictions. I think it is beautiful that people can find such choice and yet still belong to one global church: one church but with each individual local church being a different expression of the wider family of God. Rather than always being critical we need to celebrate our differences: we should appreciate the variety of music and styles, or there is an obvious danger of becoming proud and arrogant.

During my first twelve years as a Christian I was too often negative and critical of the church. I was discontented and often considered moving elsewhere. Some weeks I didn't like the music or songs; other weeks it was the sermon or a leadership decision. Church had to be 'my way' with the style and fashion I liked (notice how much of my frustration was born out of what 'I' wanted). That all changed with one text from the Bible. I was a house group leader at that time and our church was facing the challenge of a new building project. The church members were nervous about the costs involved, and this put pressure on Amanda and me when people asked for our views. Even within our house group we had some people in favour of the build while others were opposed. I was praying to God regarding a topic for the new house group season, when I came across a verse in Ephesians where Paul writes these words: 'Husbands, love your wives, just as Christ loved the Church and gave himself up for her' (5:25). That one verse blew me away. I had read it a dozen times but had always looked at it in the context of marriage. Now God was showing me something different and it changed me. This was the message: 'Love church, just as Christ loved the church and gave himself for it.'

So I made it our theme for the whole year in house group: to love church, to see church as Jesus sees it and not with our own critical eyes. We decided to try to see the positive in everything rather than the negative. We would speak well of church, seeing the potential and avoiding divisiveness and gossip. We invested in the church prayerfully and practically. One verse of Scripture changed my whole outlook on church for ever. Now I absolutely love church and I can see Jesus working through it in the most amazing ways.

This week I was chatting to Chris, the caretaker in my church. His son died at just twenty-three years of age and today as I write it is two years since his death. I asked Chris what church has meant to him over the last few years. He called it his 'home', 'a place of friendship where there is love and support'.

The church has an important role to play in our communities, sharing the love of God in very practical ways, helping those in need, as well as leading people into a relationship with Jesus and assisting them on the journey of life. Church also has a responsibility to be a place of instruction by giving us a road map for our lives. Because of this, communication is of paramount importance (something we will look at in the next chapter). Tragically, so many people today have misunderstood the message of Jesus because of poor communication.

Someone asked me if I were to start a church what would it look like? I said I would want it to be like Barry's. Barry's is Northern Ireland's premier theme park. If you picture Disneyworld on a slightly smaller scale you have a good description of Barry's. Perhaps that is a little bit of an exaggeration, but to a three-year-old child, Barry's is actually *better* than Disneyland because there are no queues or tornado storms! Barry's, in truth, is a travelling amusement park that forgot to travel and has spent the last eighty-five years in the same place. This summer Amanda and I and our two kids, Noah and Megan, went to Barry's. There were all kinds of people there enjoying themselves: rich and poor, Protestant and Catholic (you can tell by their football shirts!), young and old, large and small, and they were all having a blast. I saw a firefighter I know from Central Station along with a grandmother and granddaughter in matching purple and white shell suits (honest), and not ten yards behind them walked Jimmy Nesbitt and his family. Jimmy is a famous local actor and known to most for his roles in the dramas *Cold Feet* and *Murphy's Law*. He used to work on the big dipper at Barry's as a teenager.

That's the kind of church I would like. A place where all kinds of people from different backgrounds and cultures could come along and enjoy themselves in a safe place, where each person felt they belonged and were loved. I want church to be fun as well as challenging, educational as well as a place to relax with good coffee in big mugs. I want chocolate HobNobs not Rich Tea biscuits. (You can tell a lot about a church by its biscuits;

in fact I think if churches stopped buying Rich Tea biscuits they would go out of production!) I want church with the principles of the early church in Acts 4:32–35 as its core values:

> All the believers were one in heart and mind. No-one claimed that any of their possessions was their own, but they shared everything they had. With great power the apostles continued to testify to the resurrection of the Lord Jesus, and much grace was upon them all. There were no needy persons among them. For from time to time those who owned lands or houses sold them, brought the money from the sales and put it at the apostles' feet, and it was distributed to anyone who had need.

5. Knocking on the door: Hearing the right message

Max was in charge of my fire engine at Knock on 20 February 2002. I liked Max and had first worked with him as a firefighter seven years previously when I left the training school. Owing to promotion he had recently joined our watch on a temporary post. Max looks like he drinks whiskey and lives on a ship with a few pirates and a dog, but he doesn't. He lives with his lovely wife, Kay, in a house and he drinks beer. He does have a dog though. We were in the fire station and I was eating: I don't remember what I was eating but it's safe to say I was eating because that's what I normally do on duty. Explorer Mike Stroud, I believe, holds the record of having expended 11,650 calories in one day during a gruelling trek over Antarctica,[1] but I must hold the record for eating 11,650 calories in one day while on duty. If eating was an Olympic sport I would eat for Ireland and win gold!

Outside trees swayed against the grey, and strong winds threw litter across streets in a temper. When the fire call came through I remember putting on my flash hood first just to keep my bald head warm. We were turned out to a house fire in Knocknagoney, a housing estate about two miles from our station. I was the Breathing Apparatus (B.A.) team leader and Phil was my B.A. partner. Phil was a first-year firefighter and absolutely bonkers, a genius of a guy, but like many geniuses also completely wired to the moon. He is scarily fit, seriously clever, totally mad, and could stunt double for Mickey Rourke. Our Entry Control Officer (E.C.O.) was Bert. The role of an E.C.O. is to monitor the B.A. team during operations. Bert is a good firefighter and friend, but he can give you a stare that would have Hannibal Lecter running for cover. He has smallholdings with pigs and turkeys, like Hugh Fearnley-Whittingstall but in a fire kit. Once Bert sold Blue Watch a Christmas turkey that came out of the oven the size of a budgie. It wasn't his fault but they went mad and I cracked up laughing. Bert is a funny guy. Our driver once again was Harvey, which is always good as he knows the station area well, so we were not concerned with maps or directions. Harvey's mum used to serve me dinners in the school canteen, and if I had known that her big son was eventually going to be the senior man on the watch I might not have given her so much lip about the soggy chips! Harvey used to cook for the firemen and his chips were soggy too.

As we turned into the neighbourhood we could see the smoke. It was a terraced house with the upper floor burning. Strong winds were driving the fire right to left into the adjoining properties. Both fire engines pulled up outside and Max immediately requested back-up before leaving the appliance.

Max asked a woman neighbour if anyone was in the house.

'No,' she said.

'Are you sure?' asked Max.

'No,' she replied.

'No, you are not sure or no, it's empty?' he asked, looking for something more convincing.

'Yes, I think I am sure it's empty,' came an equally mixed reply.

Max didn't want to assume anything, so he instructed the B.A. wearers to get 'under air', and Phil and I reported to Bert to have our tallies logged on the board and get ready for entry. Everything was pretty straightforward. A second team went to the back of the house with a hose and Phil and I took a hose reel to the front door. I gave the hose a blast to ensure we had water and Phil opened the front door with a lever bar. Opening it was easy, but once we stepped inside the door slammed against the hose reel because of the force of a strong wind from inside the house. There was no smoke at all, but at the top of the stairs a broken window allowed the strong winds to drive heat and flames towards us. There was no sign of a backdraft or flashover, visibility was excellent and I could see the plaster falling from the walls at the side of the stairs due to the high temperature. The heat was incredible – it was like standing at the wrong end of a welder's blowtorch! In fifteen years of fire-fighting I had never felt heat quite like it. The hose-reel jet was on full spray and the heat was vaporizing the water only a few feet after leaving the branch nozzle. To make matters worse the steam from the spray was being blown back on to me. The idea of retreating is not an option a firefighter likes to consider, but I had no choice as I could feel my skin burning in the gap between the flash hood and B.A. mask. I pressed the push-to-talk button on my B.A. set and relayed a radio message to Bert outside: 'This is crazy hot, mate. Go and tell Max we can't get upstairs and are retreating to the front door.'

In my message I had made a fundamental mistake. By not using the appropriate call signs or names, my B.A. partner Phil beside me assumed that I was talking to him and not sending a radio message outside. Standing directly behind me, Phil was faced with a dilemma: should he leave me inside alone and give the message to Max or should he stay with me and ignore my request? As he was only a year into the job, what should he do? His training told him never to leave his B.A. partner, but now it appeared that his team leader had told him to go outside. Phil made the right decision, ignored my message and stayed. Thank God that he did, for within a few seconds the heat was too intense even at the door and we had to retreat outside. Had Phil left me, I would never have opened the door on my own while keeping the cooling spray up the stairs. I would also have been forced to stay inside to try to find Phil, assuming he was lost!

Once outside we literally lay on the doorstep and opened the door about four inches, just enough to put a spray into the hallway, and it was there that my flash hood moved and I received minor burns to my cheek and chin. This was unbelievable, a fire in an upstairs bedroom so intense that we could not get the downstairs door open to fight it.

Eventually the fire was tackled from the rear of the house and thankfully no-one was inside or in the adjoining property. While Phil, Bert and I serviced the B.A. sets, Phil shared with us the dilemma he had been in. I had no idea that he had thought I was talking to him. Once we had serviced the sets we walked inside and saw the paint blistered on the inside of the front door, yet little smoke damage.

On the way home I reflected on the incident: a poorly communicated message from a neighbour and a misunderstood message between Phil and me could have had very serious consequences. I felt that I had been *snatched from the fire*.

* * *

Rewind a bit and I am eight years old. The three Mitchell brothers were packed into the back of the family Vauxhall Viva and sent to Sunday school as usual. At 3 o'clock on a Sunday afternoon this is an absolutely appalling idea. It was worse than League of Church Loyalty or big windows in church, and to add insult to injury Sunday afternoon television included *Ski Sunday*, *Match of the Day* and *Snooker World Championships*. This was also my chance to play outside before the start of a new school week. I was no sooner home from the morning church service and given my Sunday dinner before being bundled back into my 'Sunday clothes' and down the road again to Sunday school. Sunday clothes were another reason to complain. (I'm on a roll so let me get it out of my system.) My Sunday clothes consisted of hand-me-downs from my two older brothers and Mummy's choice from my wardrobe. Let me break this down:

Shoes. Mum would always take me to the same shoe shop because she knew the lady who worked there. This was the only shoe shop that measured your feet and afterwards gave you a pair of shoes that didn't fit. 'He will grow into them,' the shoe-shop lady would say, but I never did have the chance – nine months later when they began to fit me, the toe would be ripped out because they were so big and I would be back in for yet another pair that were two sizes too big. So on Sundays I walked differently from the other days with soles never broken in so they didn't bend, and I would catch my toes on the ground.

Trousers. Now I vividly remember my mum buying me a pair of he-will-grow-into-them brown trousers to match my he-will-grow-into-them shoes. These were tacked at the bottom with pins until my mum got matching thread. The first Sunday was murder. They were made of tweed or camel's pubic hair, but either way they tore at my legs like a Brillo pad while my ankle got a free acupuncture session. Mum said my legs would get used to them, but after three weeks of pain and dozens of layers of skin being removed she finally conceded. I would wear my pyjama bottoms under my trousers. Now my legs looked like the Hulk's, and with the pyjamas being hand-me-downs from my brother they were longer than the trousers!

Jacket. I believe the jacket was a hand-me-down from another family. It was green and had corduroy flaps on the 'pockets'. I put pockets in those little flying commas for good reason. This was a lying jacket: it gave you the impression that it had pockets but it didn't – just those little flaps and nothing underneath. I thought this was stupid and very deceitful; obviously the tailor never went to Sunday school. If I was making a jacket I would do the opposite. I would make one that looked like it had no pockets but had secret pockets, and then you could hide your sweets in them!

Tie. Now my tie was the stuff of legend. If my publisher had permitted me to put in pictures, I would show you one of me wearing this tie. It was pink. Now my mother told me that it was salmon but I assure you it was pink. It was also paisley-patterned to match my pyjama bottoms and about four inches wide, and from the 'knot' about eight inches in length. Aha! I use those flying commas again over the word 'knot'. And, yes, you've guessed it, a lying knot to match my lying pockets. The tie was actually on elastic and this went under my collar, giving the impression to all and sundry that it was a real tie when it was actually something else. My brothers would pull this pink elastic thing away from my neck and then let go, sending the 'knot' zooming back and snapping against my chin. I wondered if it was the same guy behind the jacket and the tie? What else did he make? I thought about my mate, Barry, who boasted of having a second car at his house but no-one ever saw it move. Maybe my tailor had got into the automobile industry after seeing a gap in the market and was producing cars that didn't have engines but sat outside your house to impress the neighbours so you could claim you were a 'two-car family'!

So there I was walking into Sunday school in big he-will-grow-into-them shoes, hand-me-down, pyjama-lined, he-will-grow-into-them trousers and a lying jacket with a matching lying tie. I looked like a clown while Dad sat at home watching Franz Klammer race downhill on skis. Now here is the funny bit: they expected me to come in happy, singing songs and behaving like an angel!

Mr Beasley was my Sunday school teacher. His daughter Fiona was in my group and we sat in a little circle with about six others all dressed like morons. I am very thankful to all my Sunday school teachers: Mrs Busby, Mrs Haire and Mrs Hanna to name just a few. They worked wonders with the piano, felt boards and picture books. I also went to a Good News Club, a midweek house meeting organized by a couple who lived in my neighbourhood, and I liked these because I didn't have to wear my Sunday clothes. Hand-me-down clothes, though, were unfortunately unavoidable: my brother may have looked cool in tartan trousers during the Bay City Rollers' era, but now I looked more like Rupert Bear walking to the Good News Club!

One particular Sunday Mr Beasley seemed to be struggling to get our attention, and I think he possibly detoured from the script. Down went the photocopies and storyboard and he asked us to fold our arms and listen. Of all the instructions I have ever received at home, in school and in church the message that he shared that day has somehow got locked into my head. I may not be able to recall it entirely word for word but this is how I remember it:

> 'Boys and girls, I want you to listen to me like you've never listened before, for this is very important.' The hall was filled with other groups talking, laughing, drawing and shouting, but I homed in, not wanting to miss anything.
>
> 'Jesus is knocking at the door of your heart, and he wants to come in. Only you can open the door and let him in, and as you get older you may not hear him knock on the door of your heart as much as you hear him now.'

I didn't have a clue what he was talking about: a door to my heart?[2] What did he mean when he said I might not hear that knock as clearly when I got older?

Mr Beasley left me with more questions than answers that day, but I am so glad he took the time to communicate that important message to me. At times during my teenage years I would wake up on a Sunday morning with a hangover, vomit running down the side of my bed and recall how the night before I had staggered up the cul-de-sac drunk only to find my mother waiting for me in the porch. I would swear at her up and down the house some nights, but the mornings filled me with guilt as I would often ask myself, 'Is Jesus still knocking on the door of my heart? Has Jesus given up on me?'

Of course now I understand the message Mr Beasley communicated to me and I am so grateful he devoted his Sunday afternoons to sharing God's love with kids like me. Could Jesus have given up on me? At nineteen I became a Christian. Was this my last chance? I don't know the answer for sure but I do know this: there were many other things beginning to knock at the door of my heart and wanting to come in. Money, success, girlfriends and alcohol all wanted a place in my heart. Four things will rap on the door of every man's heart: gold, glory, girls and God. The first three will come in and fight for their place for the rest of your life; the other will only enter alone.

* * *

Often people will run a mile from Christianity and all of its claims simply because the message has been miscommunicated to them. 'There is nothing quite so wonderful as a good idea; there is nothing so tragic as a good idea which cannot be communicated,' according to Donald Ely.[3] Television, parents, peers, other Christians and the church have all contributed to people having a messed-up view. However, communication is also about listening, and often it is not only the source but also the receiver that is part of the problem. And some people only hear what they want to hear! Communication is a two-way process of transmission and reception and has three essential elements. The source (the one giving the message), the environment (anything from a noisy concert hall to a quiet café) and the receiver (the person for whom the message is intended). Additional factors such as timing, mood, circumstances and previous experiences of the message all play a part in the process. The benefits of effective communication are many as they enhance all aspects of our lives. Ineffective or misunderstood communication in our personal lives may give rise to problems or embarrassment. In our professional lives the results of misunderstandings may have much more serious consequences, as I discovered at the fire call. Language, accent, jargon, slogans, grammar and simply not saying what we mean or meaning what we say all complicate the message.

Now this may all sound very boring but I am gearing up to a very important point. Here is a 'Dear Jack' letter written twice, which shows the consequences of poor punctuation and how it can powerfully alter a message:

Dear Jack,
I want a man who knows what love is all about. You are
generous, kind, thoughtful. People who are not like you admit
to being useless and inferior. You have ruined me for other
men. I yearn for you. I have no feelings whatsoever when we're
apart. I can be forever happy – will you let me be yours?
Jill

Dear Jack,
I want a man who knows what love is. All about you are
generous, kind, thoughtful people, who are not like you. Admit
to being useless and inferior. You have ruined me. For other
men I yearn! For you I have no feelings whatsoever. When we're
apart I can be forever happy. Will you let me be?
Yours
Jill[4]

The secret of good communication is to minimize any distortions and distractions so that the receiver understands what the source intends to say. Punctuation, body language and vocal intonation can in many cases say more than our words. For example, we can struggle to receive a message if it is mumbled, communicated without eye contact and accompanied by agitated gestures. Good feedback is also an essential part of communication, helping the source know whether or not the message is being understood. This can be difficult with books and sermons and so they are not always the best way to communicate. Often people will avoid feedback for fear of criticism or debate, which will demand more of their time.

The church is a good example of a 'company' that is in the business of presenting an important message but has been generally poor at the feedback system. It does a lot of talking and not much listening, and as a result the truth and power of the message suffer and become distorted. We used to play a game in school called Chinese Whispers, in which one person would relay accurate information to someone in a whisper without any feedback or clarification. This is then passed on to the next person, and by the time the information is passed around twenty people the message changes completely.

And sometimes people just don't want to listen! Imagine a doctor having the cure for cancer but the patient doesn't want to discover how to take the drugs. This could be due to a bad experience of the doctor or the promise of a cure, previous drugs having failed, the dodgy reputation of the pharmaceutical company supplying the drugs or a warning from others about possible side effects. This is exactly the difficulty Christians have when sharing their faith. Christians believe they have a cure for the world's biggest problem: sin. However, the listener does not want to receive the message because they have issues with: the person wanting to communicate (they are hypocrites), the claim of Jesus being God, the company supplying the message (either the church or a particular denomination) and possible side effects (How will I respond to the message? What impact will it have on me? On my family? On my finances?).

This is no small challenge! To get someone's attention on a subject that they have already dismissed owing to previous experience is very difficult. But this is exactly what I have set out to do with this book. More than anything else, I don't want anyone to miss the joy of knowing Jesus because of the carelessness or failure of someone else.

A miscommunicated message can also be very funny. One of my favourites was a sign spotted in an office toilet:

TOILET OUT OF ORDER. PLEASE USE THE FLOOR BELOW.

However, a miscommunicated message can also have disastrous consequences. A sentence used by the British during the Second World War neatly sums up the dangers of ineffective communication: 'Careless talk costs lives.'

And here is my point: have you misunderstood the message of Jesus? Have you allowed your prejudices to influence what you have heard or read? In a court of law a member of a jury is asked not to form any preconceptions, to be open-minded and fair, drawing conclusions not based upon whims or negative opinions. I think that is a good way for everyone to approach the next chapter, for, after all, there is more than simple curiosity hanging in the balance. If Jesus really is who he claimed to be, then how we respond is the most important decision we will ever make. There are much better and wiser people out there to share the message of Jesus, but this is my contribution, my witness statement – and it may just be the key to open the door of your heart to Jesus.

Here's a paraphrase of Colossians 4:4 which sums up my prayer and my passion: 'Pray that every time I open my mouth or put pen to paper I'll be able to make Christ plain as day to everyone.'

6. Coffee:
The Passion of the Christ

I am passionate about good coffee. The Greeks launched a thousand ships for Helen of Troy but I would launch ten thousand for a good coffee. In the office everyone knows that's how I like to start my day, with fresh coffee. I think the Bible goes well with coffee and chocolate. It doesn't really matter to me what kind of chocolate I eat but the coffee does matter. I try to avoid instant stuff because for me this is not coffee at all; it's some other drink that can taste like gravy all gone wrong.

I ordered it on the flight to London when I was just looking for something warm and wet to wash down my chocolate muffin. I put the coffee on the tray at about 25,000 feet and removed the lid to add a little sugar before putting the lid back on again. Big mistake! I then lifted the cup by the lid, which was not on tightly, and 300ml of hot coffee spilled over my trousers and T-shirt. I was roasted but clenched my teeth to avoid screaming. Sitting beside me was a business lady who peered over the top of her magazine to make sure none of the brown mess had touched her Louis Vuitton handbag. The hot liquid burned my legs and I could feel it soaking into my pants from the front to the back. I was now sitting in a warm puddle, trying to be as composed as possible while wiping my jeans in vain with a single paper napkin. I sat there considering my options. This was the start of a long journey to California, and my jeans, T-shirt and pants were soaked through, which was not a good start. If I were to stand up and move I would drip coffee all over the lady and possibly make a scene. So I decided that the best option was to sit where I was beside the window in my puddle and enjoy the chocolate chip muffin . . . It was sixteen hours later when I got those pants off!

I was on my way to California for breakfast with some friends when I spilled that coffee. We were flying to London Heathrow from Belfast before boarding a connecting flight to Los Angeles. I know what you are thinking: California is a long way to go for breakfast, and would Tesco or IKEA not serve you a good breakfast for a lot less money and travel? True, but a good breakfast is more than food. It's about the people you connect with while you eat, and that's another thing I'm passionate about: connecting with others. Orange County, California was the venue for the annual Firefighters For Christ International breakfast, and a team of six from Northern Ireland were making the pilgrimage for more than a hash brown, sausage and coffee. We wanted to encourage our American counterparts and support their efforts to reach other firefighters with the good news of Jesus.

This was my fifth visit to California and, although the visit was primarily for the breakfast, I was staying a little longer than my colleagues in order to speak at a meeting in Fresno and also to catch up with some great friends in the Redondo Beach area.

During my two-week stay there was a lot of talk about the new Mel Gibson movie due to be launched in the local cinemas. The press were going wild for interviews with church leaders, Jews and politicians, looking for a view or opinion on the release of what was described by one editor as a 'controversial masterpiece'. Back in Northern Ireland, people were keen to see the reaction in America, and the local church was curious to find out if this was a movie to recommend or avoid. It would be almost two months before the UK release and being in America for the opening week was an opportunity I didn't want to miss. The movie of course was *The Passion of the Christ*.

I invited my friend Campbell along, hoping that the movie would spark meaningful conversation afterwards. Campbell and his wife are two of the nicest people I have ever met and although not professing Christians they are open to the ideas and teachings of Jesus. The cinema had twelve screens and as it turned out every screen was showing *The Passion of the Christ*! The only viewing we could get was for 2 pm on the Thursday afternoon, and even with a ticket the lady at the box office recommended that we arrive almost two hours before the scheduled start. Campbell and I arrived just over one hour before the start time and already there was a queue around the block. We moved into our seats and a Mexican family sat beside us. The youngest child was perhaps eight years old and, given the hype about the brutality of what we were about to watch, I was uneasy about the effect it might have on her.

The movie got off to a good start. When Jesus stood on the snake (representing Satan) in the garden I wanted to jump out of my seat and whoop and yehaa as if the Lakers had just won the NBA![1] But soon the movie became dark and brutal. Just when you thought you had seen Jesus endure enough beatings, it started again. At points I simply could not look at the screen any more. The tears were rolling down my face, and when the whip caught the back of Jesus in a relentless attack I wanted to stand up and shout, 'Stop! Stop beating him, stop beating my friend.' I was an emotional mess during the movie and afterwards. I felt like I was there, that his blood was on me and that I needed to take a shower. All my intentions to discuss the movie and the message of Jesus with Campbell had disappeared. We both left the cinema feeling numb: what had we just watched? I felt that I had become a witness to the most brutal crime in the history of mankind – when man kills his Maker. Campbell didn't know what to say or ask and so we just drove quietly back to his place. I went into my room, closed the door, knelt by my bed, prayed and wept some more. I knew people would be asking me my opinion and I didn't know how to process what I had seen. I opened my journal and wrote the following:

Date: 2–28–04 (I was in America, remember!)
At some points during the movie I thought 'the world needs to see this', whilst at other times I felt 'the world doesn't need to see this'. I have just sat through an emotional roller coaster and don't know if I want to ride it ever again!
    I need to remind myself that this is not the gospel, but rather it is Mel Gibson's response to the gospel in the way he knows best, through the big screen. God has used Mel Gibson's talent to bring the message of Jesus to the world. Is it accurate? About as accurate as some of my preaching which is just my response to the gospel, so who am I to judge?

It took some weeks before I was prepared to recommend the movie to others. I struggled with the idea of suggesting to someone that they needed to go and see my best friend being beaten to death. It was only a movie, of course, an enactment of Jesus' death, but it felt so real and personal to me. In the end I adopted the recommendations that Pastor Rick Warren gave to his congregation in Saddleback:

You should see this movie for three reasons:

1. It is a cinematic masterpiece, a work of art;
2. It is one of the greatest evangelistic opportunities you may ever have; millions of people are gossiping the gospel;
3. It is a movie about the greatest moment and the greatest character in history.

* * *

The word 'passion' can be traced back to an Old English phrase used in 1175 referring to 'the sufferings of Christ on the cross'. Central to the Christian message are the suffering, death and resurrection of Jesus Christ. I am passionate about this passion. If this did not happen, then my faith is nonsense and I would be better spending my time with my family and enjoying coffee and chocolate with some book other than the Bible. The cross is not only the primary symbol of Christianity, but the place where our whole faith hangs like weights upon a scale. In the Christian account, Jesus, the Son of God, dies so that God can forgive our sins. However, many people suggest that Jesus was not the Son of God but rather a good moral teacher or a political revolutionary. Others agree with comedian Billy Connolly that he must have been 'a wonderful man'. It may surprise you to know that there are still others who believe Jesus is just a figment of someone's imagination. This however raises more questions than answers. Why did so many people die for a lie? Even today Christians are perse-cuted for their beliefs to the extent of death in many countries. Why did the Romans and Jews not stamp out the message of Jesus? If the Gospels were mere novels then this would be easy, but it seems that the writers were reporters 'on the ground' covering the story. Before everyone's eyes, the very traditions and customs of the time were being changed by their reports!

Today even the date on the newspapers points to the life of Jesus. If Jesus was just a figment of someone's imagination, then who preached the message known as 'the Sermon on the Mount', one of the greatest texts ever to be recorded? The evidence for the life of Jesus outside the Bible is also very powerful. Records from Josephus,[2] Tacitus,[3] Pliny the Younger[4] and others affirm the Gospels along with the finds from many archaeological digs. Jesus is more than a fantasy character from the imagination and certainly not on the same plane as the tooth fairy.

So was Jesus the Son of God or just a good teacher? According to Mark's Gospel, Jesus is asked by the high priest, 'Are you the Christ, the Son of the Blessed One?' (14:61).

The Jews had been waiting for the Christ for hundreds of years and they were expecting him to arrive as a king, to conquer the Romans, bring liberty to Israel and enforce the laws of God. But Jesus stood before them as a suffering servant, a carpenter's son from Nazareth, a young man in his early thirties who arrived in Jerusalem on a donkey! He seemed to be causing confusion among the Jews, not just by condemning but by challenging and mocking their traditions and laws. On top of that he backed up his claims with what seemed to be some wonderful magic tricks: feeding thousands, calming the seas and opening blind eyes, to name just a few.

The question is put to him, 'Are you the Christ, the Son of the Blessed One?' He replies, 'I am, and you will see the Son of Man [a reference to himself] sitting at the right hand of the Mighty One and coming on the clouds of heaven' (Mark 14:62).

The crowds went mad. This wasn't just a deluded man, the local nutcase or village idiot whom everyone could pat on the head saying, 'Poor Jesus, he's out of his mind.' No, this was a man who posed a serious threat, with hundreds of people already following his teachings.

Let me give you a little bit of advice. If anyone should ever come up to you and introduce themselves as God, you have three options:

1. Ignore them for they are liars and dangerous and probably after your money.

2. Forgive them for they have a diminished capacity and need some medical help.
3. Follow and worship them for they *are* God.

Jesus' claim to be the Son of God therefore forces a decision from us: he is either the Son of God or a lunatic or a liar. For the Jews he was a liar and a DANGER.

The Jewish leaders demanded that Jesus be put to death by crucifixion, an agonizing and public death by torture. The victim would be in excruciating pain; indeed, the very word 'excruciating' means 'from the cross'. The Romans would eventually ban this form of death because it was so inhumane.

So how did Jesus die? I have read not only the Bible but other books on the subject.

After a sleepless night and trials by Jewish and Roman leaders, Jesus was exhausted. Indeed, prior to the trials we read that in a garden called Gethsemane Jesus was agonizing over his torture and death so much that he sweated drops of blood (Luke 22:44). This condition is known as hematidrosis and occurs when the body is subject to high psychological stress. According to the medical dictionary it occurs when there is a breakdown in the capillaries, and blood and sweat mix, making the skin fragile and sensitive. It requires 'immediate medical attention'.

Before being sentenced to death Jesus is slapped and punched, his beard (a sign of a Jewish man's dignity and maturity) ripped from his face, a crown of long thorns placed on his head as he is beaten with sticks. The people mock him saying, 'Hail, King of the Jews'. They blindfold him, hit him with sticks and ask, 'Who hit you, Jesus?' Already weak and weary, he then endures a Roman flogging administered with a cat-o'-nine-tails, a leather whip often with pieces of lead and bone woven in to bruise and tear the flesh. A third-century historian,

Eusebius, describes the flogging as follows: 'The sufferer's veins were laid bare and the very muscles, sinews and bowels of the victim were open to exposure.'[5]

Jesus' body would have gone into shock; his heart rate would have risen, pumping blood that wasn't there, which in turn would have caused his blood pressure to drop, resulting in fainting, dizziness and thirst. Then his kidneys and other vital organs would have begun to stop functioning.

Before an angry crowd Jesus now stands in his final trial. A scarlet robe hangs and sticks upon his bleeding and broken frame. As the crowd cry 'Crucify him, crucify him,' I have often wondered what words he whispered to his heavenly Father.

In 1896 Mihály Munkácsy, a Hungarian artist, painted a powerful picture entitled *Ecce Homo*, 'Behold the man', which depicts Jesus before the crowd and Pilate giving the people the choice to release or crucify him. It's a powerful picture showing some people shaking fists and shouting while others appear to be weeping and turning away.

Pilate, the crowd-pleasing coward, hands Jesus over to be crucified. He releases Barabbas, a criminal and enemy of Rome, to the angry mob. Jesus is forced to carry a large wooden cross through the city, and only when his strength has left him do they force an observer to carry it. Finally they reach the Hill of Golgotha. There his arms are stretched out on to the wooden cross-beam before a spike is hammered between the wrist bones, crushing the median nerve, shooting pain through his body. His knees are bent and his ankles twisted, before a spike is driven in, pressing them against a wooden post. The cross is then lifted up and dropped into a hole in the ground, and Jesus is left to die in the heat of the day. In order to take a breath he would have to push down on his feet, releasing the pressure in the chest cavity before falling again due to the pain in his ankles and feet. This action of rising and falling continues until the victim becomes unconscious. If they want to hasten the death the soldiers break the legs of the victim so that he cannot push up to get a breath.

After six hours on the cross, Jesus cries out, 'It is finished' and dies. Cause of death: respiratory acidosis leading to asphyxiation, carbon dioxide in the blood leading to an irregular heartbeat before suffocation. Heart failure of this kind would cause the heart to burst.

Now you may call it symbolic, but Jesus died of a broken heart.

But why? Why did Jesus have to die? If God is so powerful, could he not just leave out this torture bit and forgive us without the mess and the pain?

7. Arthur the gardener: God's amazing grace

When I was a teenager 'Arthur the gardener' got a motorbike for his birthday. He had been saving up for ages and now with a little help from his parents he purchased his very first bike. He had turned sixteen, now the legal age to ride the motorbike. I was delighted for him but thought I would play a little joke. I waited until he parked the bike outside the local sweet shop, and while he was inside I took the bike for a spin along the footpath next to a busy dual carriageway – not a good idea! Soon the sound of the siren and the sight of blue lights dancing in the wing mirrors suggested it might be a good time to call an end to the little joke.

The police officer was tall, thin and spotty and had ginger hair. His uniform was neatly pressed and it looked like it was his first day on the job. He wasted no time in putting on his cap before reading the riot act to me, spelling out my rights over and over again as he highlighted the charges against me:

- No helmet
- No licence
- No insurance
- Under age
- Riding on the footpath
- No tax on the bike (I told him that was not my fault but he didn't listen)
- Riding a stolen bike (Arthur had arrived at the scene and wasted no time sinking me in it)
- Careless driving

By the time he had finished I thought I was going to spend the rest of my life in jail, probably Alcatraz!

Because I was just fifteen the juvenile liaison officer and 'ginger cop' came out to our home. They had to discuss how I might be punished for my actions. Mum suggested that I stay out of the house in case I made matters worse. She met with the officers and, although I don't know the full extent of the conversation, I imagine my mum said I was a good boy and explained how she had been recently widowed and had three teenage boys. Mum would not have defended my actions but she did emphasize that I was very sorry.

When I came home I was amazed to find that the police would keep a record of the incident on file but take no legal action, provided I was disciplined at home. I gave a sigh of relief and was happy to wash dishes and do a few extra duties round the house. The officers were good to me, accepting my apology and the sincerity of my mother, but there still had to be a penalty. The officer could not write on his report, 'No action taken'. That would have been negligence on his part, and so my mother was responsible for handing out an appropriate punishment and the officers were happy that this could be done at home.

I have already highlighted that none of us is perfect. The Bible says that we have all fallen from God's standards and calls this 'sin'. Now when someone commits a crime the law demands justice. Either you absorb the cost of the deed or someone else does, but the debt cannot just vanish into thin air! God cannot just declare, 'No action taken' and let us go free. To do this is to discard the law, making it nonsensical and making God unjust.

This is the good news of Christianity: that Jesus Christ takes the punishment you and I deserve, and, in doing so, we go free. He became our substitute, and in that one act of compassion and mercy God is satisfied that the debt has been paid and we are forgiven. Forgiveness is won because Jesus bears the cost instead of making the wrongdoer bear it. Forgiveness means cancelling out the debt of sin, and that's exactly what Jesus did.

But why did he die such a cruel death? Because he absorbed the sins of the world, dying for every sin, past, present and future, and that includes yours and mine. He died for mass murderers, sex offenders and child abusers, as well as those who have committed 'smaller' crimes like stealing a pencil from school. He took the punishment you and I deserve. The Bible says, 'God made him who had no sin to be sin for us, so that in him we might become the righteousness of God' (2 Corinthians 5:21). He took my sin and in return I receive his righteousness. What a swap!

When I was a kid we used to watch a programme on Saturday mornings called *Multi-Coloured Swap Shop*, presented by Noel Edmonds. You could phone in to the show and agree to swap something for someone else's goods. For example, you could offer to swap your toy car for a Chelsea football scarf. The items had to be a reasonable like-for-like offer in order to clinch a deal. But here is God 'phoning in' and offering everyone his righteousness for our filthy sins! He takes our hell so that we can enter heaven.

The Bible is very clear that beyond this life your soul will live on in one of two places: either heaven or hell. Hell was designed for Satan and his demons and the good news is that God will send no-one to hell. The bad news is we can send ourselves there. By rejecting God's plan, his offer of eternal life and his love, we choose to pay the penalty for our sin. We take the consequences for our decision. The Bible describes hell as a place of unsuitable company, unhappy memories, everlasting torment, unsatisfied desires and a rubbish dump of flames. Heaven on the other hand is described as a place where there are no more tears, pain, sorrow, death or darkness. It is the garden of God, a celestial city, and best of all the dwelling place of God.

Now for everyone who reads this chapter recognizing that they are sinners, this message is good news: God loves you so much that he gave his Son as a ransom for you. If you had been the only person in the world, Jesus would have died for you. This is not a fictional story about someone else that moves our emotions; it is a story about you and me. The Romans or the Jews didn't kill Jesus – you and I did! I am told that in *The Passion of the Christ*, when it came to nailing Jesus to the cross, Mel Gibson stepped in and took the hammer. He was making a statement: it wasn't someone else who killed him – it was you and me.

In his dying breath Jesus cried, *'Tetelestai'* ('It is finished' or 'paid in full'), a powerful statement meaning that there is nothing you and I can bring to the cross other than our sin. There is no way of earning his love or adding to his work, nothing that we can do to clean ourselves up. In that one act of love, Jesus brings us into a right relationship with God, cleanses us from our sin, frees us from guilt and places heaven in our heart.

Fiorello LaGuardia was Mayor of New York City during some of the worst days of the Great Depression and all of the Second World War. He was adoringly called 'the Little Flower' by the people of New York because he stood only five feet four and always wore a carnation in his lapel.

He was a colourful character. Sometimes he would ride the New York City fire trucks or go with the police when they raided the speakeasies. He would take entire orphanages to a baseball game. Once he went on radio during a newspaper strike and read comics to the children.

One really cold night in January 1935 he showed up at night court in the poorest ward of the city and dismissed the judge for the evening, taking over the bench himself. A tattered old woman was brought before him. She was charged with stealing a loaf of bread. Her daughter was sick and her grandchildren starving. But the shopkeeper from whom she stole the bread refused to drop the charges, stating, 'It's a real bad neighbour-hood, Your Honour. She's got to be punished to teach other people around here a lesson.'

LaGuardia sighed as if deep in thought. Finally, he turned to the woman and said, 'I've got to punish you. The law makes no exceptions – ten dollars or ten days in jail.'

But even as he was pronouncing the sentence he was reaching into his pocket. He took out a ten-dollar bill and tossed it into his famous sombrero saying, 'Here is the ten-dollar fine which I now remit, and furthermore I am going to fine everyone in this courtroom fifty cents for living in a town where a person has to steal bread so that her grandchildren can eat. Mr Bailiff, collect the fines and give them to the defendant.'

The following day the newspapers reported that $47.50 was turned over to the bewildered woman who had stolen a loaf of bread to feed her starving grandchildren, fifty cents of it being contributed by the red-faced grocery store owner, while the remainder came from some seventy petty criminals, people with traffic violations, and New York City police officers, each of whom paid fifty cents and then gave the mayor a standing ovation.[1]

What a wonderful picture of grace (unmerited favour).

Grace is amazing because it goes against every grain of common sense. It warms our heart to read this story but we can be too proud to receive grace ourselves. Pride is all too often our biggest stumbling block. We do not want to admit we have been wrong; we are too proud to say sorry, too stubborn to ask God for help and too proud to lean upon him.

Common sense reminds us that we are unable to meet the standards of a holy God – too weak, too harassed, too human to change for the better. Grace births within us the power to send us on our way to being better people despite all we know that is wrong within ourselves. And this is no cheap grace because it cost Jesus his life.

If you reject the grace of Jesus how else will you be free from your sin? Who else will pay the punishment you deserve? Do you think you can save yourself? Max Lucado says:

> The conclusion is unavoidable: self-salvation simply does not work. Man has no way to save himself.
>
> But Paul announces that God has a way. Where man fails God excels. Salvation comes from heaven downward, not earth upward. 'A new day from heaven will dawn upon us' (Luke 1:78). 'Every good action and every perfect gift comes from God' (James 1:17).
>
> Please note: salvation is God-given, God-driven, God-empowered, and God-originated. The gift is not from man to God. It is from God to man.
>
> Grace is created by God and given to man . . . On the basis of this point alone, Christianity is set apart from any other religion in the world . . . Every other approach to God is a bartering system: If I do this, God will do that. I'm either saved by works (what I do), emotions (what I experience), or knowledge (what I know).
>
> By contrast, Christianity has no whiff of negotiation at all. Man is not the negotiator; indeed, man has no grounds from which to negotiate.[2]

Is God working in your life right now? If you haven't done so for a while or perhaps ever, pray and talk to Jesus. Thank him for dying on the cross for your sins and ask him to forgive you for self-addiction. Ask him to become real to you. He's not dead but alive.

8. Alive:
Exploding some myths

I was never what you would have called a 'baby person'. I didn't dance with excitement at the sight of a new baby, neither did I ask their weight or what time they were born at and I certainly didn't huff if I didn't get a cuddle. Babies all looked the same to me and behaved the same: they ate, slept, cried and pooed. If a friend or family member had a baby I would do well to remember the sex and name. To be honest all the hype was just wasted on me.

When my wife became pregnant with our son, all that began to change as something slowly began to awaken in me. I'll call it my paternal instinct as I'm not sure what else to call it, but it was a nice warm feeling mixed with responsibility and duty. I would ride my motorcycle and all of a sudden feel that my family could suffer if I had an accident. I began to watch baby programmes on TV and even read books on fatherhood. I asked pastors and church leaders for advice on managing my time between family and ministry. I liked the changes that were happening but I was also a little anxious: how would I cope with sleepless nights and nappies? My dad, so I am told, never changed a nappy even once on his three sons. How times have changed! Now a man is expected to fulfil all the duties of a woman with the exception of breast-feeding (thank God!). Apart from Lemon in Romania I had never changed a nappy, and that was just a wet one. What would I do with a stinker? There was every chance I would vomit all over the baby.

The ultrasound scan at fourteen weeks blew me away. Some people told me I would see the baby's head and body; others said I might not see much, just a grey blob. Marcus Berkmann writes in *Fatherhood* that 'this looks like a photocopy of a photocopy of an artist's impression of a stoat', so I didn't go with any great expectations. All I wanted was a doctor to say that mother and baby were doing fine. But baby Noah decided to put on a show for Mummy and Daddy. We could see his hands, arms, legs and the outline of a face. He wriggled and moved when we wanted him to and posed for a photo at all the right times. Now all that was very cute, but seeing the actual heartbeat left me in awe at the beauty and wonder of human life. (If this was an email I would stick a smiley face in here, but I have been told not to do that as books are not cool enough yet.) To be honest, sometimes the doctor would point at the screen and say, 'That's the baby's leg', and I would look and give a nod of agreement when I couldn't make anything out, but at other times when he froze the screen I was mesmerized as I watched the shape of our tiny baby. But the picture of the heart beating on the screen, and knowing that the baby was alive and well, just made me want to throw a party.

I have been at fire calls when the word 'Alive' has been shouted from a smoke-filled house and it brings such relief to those who are anxious for news. It's such a brilliant word. I wasn't worried before the scan but, when you see the heartbeat, in the back of your mind you are relieved and thinking, 'Thank God he/she is alive.' I remember reading of an earthquake in Turkey where everyone had lost hope of finding anyone alive. Everyone that was except the uncle of a young boy buried under the twisted metal and concrete. As the other family members wept and made preparations for the funeral, the uncle kept digging, kept hoping, kept believing. After 104 hours of removing rubble they made contact with the boy. 'He's alive,' cried the uncle, 'He's alive.' What power, joy and euphoria in that single word, 'alive'. And, of course, who could forget the euphoria when thirty-three Chilean miners were rescued after being trapped underground for almost seventy days? As images were beamed around the world there was celebration that each had been brought out alive.

At home I began doing the things that fathers-to-be are expected to do: I got the baby room ready, we went shopping for the buggy and car seat (men like this bit), I offered Amanda help with the usual household chores (men don't like this bit!) and basically stayed on top of the game, ever ready for an emergency. Eventually I also succumbed to the request to go with Amanda to antenatal classes with the agreement that if any clashed with Chelsea playing a Champions League match I was exempt from going. I just didn't see the point in all the group-session stuff. I don't recall learning anything of value but I was reminded that it was important to attend so that the mummy, daddy and baby could bond together. So there I was, rocking backwards and forwards on my butt on a wooden floor while rubbing my wife's tummy in front of a dozen other couples and a few nurses. I was much happier bonding with Mummy and baby under the twelve-tog duvet at home – I felt a right idiot! It wasn't until the last week that they allowed the future fathers to meet together in a discussion group. We were supposed to be talking through our fears of fatherhood when I suggested we just cut the nonsense and get home for the football match highlights. The nurse was shocked but the lads cracked up in laughter. It seemed we all felt the same about the class with the exception of one non-football fan. Weirdo.

My son Noah was born ten days past the due date. (One thing you can be certain of is that the estimated date of arrival is the only day in the whole nine months on which your child will not be born.) After a long labour I was exhausted (never mind Amanda!). 'You have your boy; you have your boy,' she exclaimed with joy as I wiped the tears from my face. What a powerful experience fatherhood is. Not until you have your own children (or adopt) can you really appreciate the wonder of parenthood. Our daughter Megan, born three years later, was the first girl in the Mitchell family tree after nine boys. She is adorable and I was over the moon at having what is often called a 'gentleman's family': one boy, one girl.

Our children have brought such joy to our home and I have never yet vomited at the sight of a dirty nappy. I wouldn't queue up to clean someone else's kid's butt, mind you, but when it's your own baby you don't mind. As for the lack of sleep, well that never became a problem as both our children sleep from 8 pm to 8 am regularly. In fact, since Noah was twelve weeks and Megan was six weeks old they began to sleep the whole night through. When I told some parents how good the children were at sleeping, they either assumed I was a liar or became jealous.

Parenting has shifted things inside of me. I look at babies now in prams and smile and I ask about other babies. I have even considered offering to help some Sundays in the church crèche. The miracle of it all is that my children are part of me, and watching them grow and develop makes me feel all warm and special. They smile when I come through the door and give me hugs and kisses. I feel like I belong; it makes me feel alive.

The gift of life is so very beautiful – from seeing the first heartbeat on the scan to holding the baby in your arms you are in awe. Science may be able to break it down into all kinds of processes and chemicals but you cannot get away from the joy it brings when life begins. I am not an expert in biology but Bill Bryson's brilliant book (*A Short History of Nearly Everything*) makes things simple yet absolutely fascinating for me. Let me share from the introduction:

Welcome and congratulations. I am delighted that you could make it. Getting here wasn't easy, I know. In fact, I suspect it was a little tougher than you realize. To begin with, for you to be here now trillions of drifting atoms had somehow to assemble in an intricate and intriguingly obliging manner to create you. It's an arrangement so specialized and particular that it has never been tried before and will only exist this once. For the next many years (we hope) these tiny particles will uncomplainingly engage in all the billions of deft, cooperative efforts necessary to keep you intact and let you experience the supremely agreeable but generally underappreciated state known as existence . . . Whatever else it may be, at the level of chemistry life is curiously mundane: carbon, hydrogen, oxygen, and nitrogen, a little calcium, a dash of sulfur, a light dusting of other very ordinary elements – nothing you wouldn't find in any ordinary drugstore – and that's all you need. The only thing special about the atoms that make you is that they make you. That is of course the miracle of life.[1]

The miracle of life is a wonder, but what about the idea of dying and coming back to life? Being dead, totally dead, dead as a dead thing and then all those atoms that shut you down and disassemble change their mind and decide to start you up again. Can you get your head around that? I don't want you to confuse this with NDEs (near-death experiences), those instances in which a medical professional observes that all life signs have ceased and yet they are able to resuscitate and bring the individual back to life. These NDEs are very interesting and there are many documented cases, but they are often just that – *near*-death experiences. Dead people don't usually come back to life, so some folk have a hard time with this simple statement: 'He [Jesus] is alive; he is risen.'

The claims of Christianity are about Jesus dying on the cross for our sins and three days later coming back to life. Christianity is asking us to believe that in a cold damp tomb Jesus' cheeks went from grey to pink as he came back to life. Christianity is asking us to believe that after eight hours of interrogation and brutal beatings, six hours nailed to a cross, a spear rammed into his side, that almost forty hours later, Jesus unwrapped himself from a yard of cloth soaked in a hundred pounds of spices, pushed away a large two-ton stone and appeared not only to a small band of followers but to 500 witnesses as the picture of health.[2] Now that's a big ask!

The truth is that the resurrection (being raised from the dead and coming back to life) of Jesus Christ is either one of the most wicked, vicious, heartless hoaxes ever foisted on the minds of any human being or it is the most remarkable fact of history. The apostle Paul writes this in one of his letters:

> And if Christ has not been raised from the dead, our preaching
> is useless and so is your faith . . . If Christ has not been raised,
> your faith is futile; you are still in your sins . . . If only for this
> life we have hope in Christ, we are to be pitied more than
> all people.
> (1 Corinthians 15:14–19)

The resurrection is absolutely crucial to the Christian faith. Without it the Bible is just a dead letter. A recent Rasmussen survey (April 2009) highlighted the fact that 97% of evangelical Christians in the USA believe that Jesus rose from the dead. The description 'evangelical Christian' is intended to describe a believer in Jesus Christ who is faithful in sharing and promoting the good news. Now my maths is not the best but this would indicate that 3% of evangelical Christians either do not believe or are unsure whether Jesus rose from the dead. It begs a question: what is the good news if Jesus is dead?

I'm going to attempt to answer the four main questions that people ask regarding the resurrection story. (I have omitted the suggestion that Elvis saved him, Star Trek beamed him up and David Blaine used a big mirror.)

- Did Jesus really die?
- Did the disciples hallucinate?
- Did someone steal the body?
- Was it not just legend that the tomb was empty?

Did Jesus really die?
This has been known as the 'swoon theory', that Jesus was taken from the cross before his death and that in the cold of the tomb or because of medical attention from others Jesus was 'resurrected'. Many Muslims believe this, stating that further sayings of Muhammad (outside the Koran) mention that Jesus died in Kashmir at the age of 120.

I have already highlighted the horrific torture Jesus endured. Given that the Romans were disciplined soldiers and experts in killing people, it is difficult to understand how Jesus was able to walk about three days later full of health and inspiration! A Roman soldier given the order to kill someone would carry out his job with precision. To fail in his task would risk his own punishment, even death. John records:

> Because the Jews did not want the bodies left on the crosses during the Sabbath, they asked Pilate to have the legs broken and the bodies taken down. The soldiers therefore came and broke the legs of the first man who had been crucified with Jesus, and then those of the other. But when they came to Jesus and found that he was already dead, they did not break his legs. Instead, one of the soldiers pierced Jesus' side with a spear, bringing a sudden flow of blood and water.
> (John 19:31–34)

Alexander Metherell stresses the significance of the spear:

> Even before Jesus died – and this is important, too – the
> hypovolemic shock would have caused a sustained rapid heart
> rate that would have contributed to heart failure, resulting in the
> collection of fluid in the membrane around the heart, called a
> pericardial effusion, as well as around the lungs, which is called
> a pleural effusion . . . Then the Roman soldier came around and,
> being fairly certain that Jesus was dead, confirmed it by thrusting
> a spear into his right side; that's not certain but it was probably
> his right side between the ribs. The spear apparently went
> through the right lung and into the heart, so when the spear was
> pulled out, some fluid – the pericardial effusion and the pleural
> effusion – came out. This would have had the appearance of a
> clear fluid, like water, followed by a large volume of blood, just
> as the eye witness John described in his gospel . . . There was
> absolutely no doubt that Jesus was dead.[3]

Did the disciples hallucinate?

I remember sniffing petrol one night as a teenager. Boon and I
collapsed on to grass and everything moved out of sync.
Time, perspective, reason, companions all became a blur as
something happened inside our heads. People hallucinate
independently and can't tell the difference between dreaming
and reality. Petrol is a solvent capable of dissolving grease and
fat and it dissolves the neurological pathways within a sniffer's
brain. It is very dangerous. It was a stupid, stupid thing for me
to do. I have friends who had some pretty nasty 'trips' that
affected them for many months after drug abuse: in Steven's
case he was haunted by the image of him throwing his own
heart on the ground.

Hallucinations give a false impression of reality. It is possible
for an individual to have a hallucination, but how do you get

two, three or four people to misperceive reality and claim to see the same thing at the same time? The idea of the disciples having individual hallucinations after the unexpected death of Jesus is questionable. Their hopes and dreams had suddenly been dashed. Extreme grief would have been their normal response – not the mass emotionalism that can play tricks on the mind. The wide variety of times and places when Jesus appeared, along with the differing mindsets of the witnesses, surely dismisses the hallucination theory. The accounts of men and women, hard-headed and soft-hearted alike, all believing that they saw Jesus both indoors and outdoors provides another barrier to the theory. The odds that each person would have been in precisely the proper and same frame of mind to experience a hallucination even individually is hard to believe.

Generally, hallucinations do not transform lives. Studies indicate that even those who do hallucinate often reject the experiences when others present have not seen the same thing. Even hardened critics acknowledge that Jesus' disciples were transformed even to the point of being willing to die for their faith. No-one reports that any of them ever changed their opinion, so it is highly unlikely that this quality of absolute conviction came about through hallucination.

If the appearances were hallucinations then opponents could have located Jesus' body safely and securely in his grave just outside the city of Jerusalem. That body would have undoubtedly been a rather large obstacle to the disciples' efforts to preach that Jesus had been raised! Also, why did the hallucinations stop after forty days?

I remember as a child reading Hans Christian Andersen's classic, *The Emperor's New Clothes*. It's a comical look at how someone can be fooled by the perception of others. Towards the end the emperor goes on a procession through the capital showing off his new 'clothes'. During the course of the procession, a small child cries out, 'The emperor is naked!' The crowd realizes the child is telling the truth, but the emperor holds his head high and continues his procession. Do you really think that millions of Christians are as gullible as the emperor and that we have all in ignorance lifted our heads high and continued on in our procession based on the hallucinations of a few downhearted fishermen?

Did someone steal the body?

Matthew records:

> While the women were on their way, some of the guards went into the city and reported to the chief priests everything that had happened. When the chief priests had met with the elders and devised a plan, they gave the soldiers a large sum of money, telling them, 'You are to say, "His disciples came during the night and stole him away while we were asleep." If this report gets to the governor, we will satisfy him and keep you out of trouble.' So the soldiers took the money and did as they were instructed. And this story has been widely circulated among the Jews to this very day.
> (Matthew 28:11–15)

I laugh when I read that account. Imagine with me these soldiers going to their general and repeating the story the chief priests suggested. Skin clammy and belly a bag of nerves, they try to get their story right and share it with conviction. They draw straws to decide who will speak up and the loser steps forward and clears his throat: 'While we were sleeping the disciples stole the body.'

The general sits and ponders the report, swirling his wine around the silver goblet and pausing long enough for them to feel sick with worry. Without lifting his eyes from his scarlet juice he asks, 'How do you know this since you were sleeping?' The guards look at one another, desperately trying to find a defence but aware that their story is now as watertight as Niagara Falls.

No wonder the story was so widely circulated. It must have been a household joke. I'm sure over time it was edited somewhat to start like this: 'Paddy the Irishman and Paddy the Scotsman were minding the tomb . . .

So who stole the body? Was it the Jews or the Romans? This is ridiculous to believe. The culture of the day was being turned on its head much to the frustration of both the Jews and the Romans, and all this could have been stopped if someone had produced the body.

Was it the disciples, then? The chances of a disillusioned group who had fled in fear suddenly thinking up the idea, overpowering the guards and hiding the body in some remote grave is extremely unlikely. Why would so many of them endure torture and death knowing the body was rotting away in an unmarked grave? What was it that caused them to live in such power and authority? What made Peter preach with such conviction that he saw 3,000 people converted at a single meeting (Acts 2:41)? Before Jesus' death this same guy had denied Jesus three times when asked if he was a follower (Matthew 26:69–75). Now he was shouting it from the rooftops with boldness and passion.

Was it not just legend that the tomb was empty?
In Jewish culture if you wrote a legend you would not have had two women as the first witnesses. Their testimony would not have been regarded in a Jewish court, yet all four Gospel writers say a small group of women visited the tomb early on the Sunday morning and found it empty.

It takes approximately two generations before legend can develop. There was simply too rapid a growth in Christianity in the first twenty years to put it down to legend. In fact, in less than six weeks all Jerusalem was buzzing with excitement that Jesus was alive. Within three months it was popular opinion and in twenty years approximately 125,000 people in Jerusalem were Christian. There can be no doubt that Jesus appeared to many, for how else do you account for the launch of the church, its dramatic growth, passionate preaching, and the change of the Sabbath rest day from Saturday to Sunday?

There's only one valid explanation: God raised him up.
Former Chief Justice of England Lord Darling said:

In its favour as a living truth there exists such overwhelming evidence, positive and negative, factual and circumstantial, that no intelligent jury in the world could fail to bring in a verdict that the resurrection story is true.[4]

Sir Lionel Luckhoo was a brilliant attorney whose outstanding 245 consecutive murder acquittals earned him a place in *The Guinness Book of Records* as the world's most successful lawyer. Knighted twice by Queen Elizabeth, this former justice and diplomat subjected the historical facts about the resurrection to his own rigorous analysis for several years before declaring, 'I say unequivocally that the evidence of the resurrection of Jesus Christ is so overwhelming that it compels acceptance by proof which leaves absolutely no room for doubt.'[5]

The last piece of evidence for the resurrection is the best I can offer. I have not learned it from studying books or listening to the ideas of others. I feel very passionate about this evidence and for this reason will devote a whole chapter to it. It is my personal experience and how I discovered Jesus to be the Son of God and the Saviour of the world. Millions of people like me have discovered the same: a personal relationship with Jesus.

9. Snatched from the fire: The Lord's gym

Around 2 am the lights flashed on and the alarm beeped suddenly in the station dorm. I was based in Springfield Road fire station in Belfast at the time and it was common to have a few calls during the night, usually car fires or rubbish skips. The board highlighted that both machines were requested. We dressed quickly and headed for the engine room. 'Multiple persons reported,' shouted our station officer, Gordon Graham, after reading the printout from controls. Everyone went into 'rescue mode': B.A. teams went under air, E.C.O. checked tallies and everyone made the necessary preparations so that on arrival there would be no delay. A 'multiple persons reported' had been phoned through by a number of witnesses to a house fire at the bottom of Ligoniel Road just minutes away from the station.

As we drove towards the house I could see three little heads popping out of the top opening of a window. The eldest child was no older than nine. Thick black smoke billowed out above and around their tiny heads and we knew that every second was going to count. I was three years into the job and this was a call where your training and skills can make the difference between life or death.

Ian Crow parked the appliance and screamed for a ladder crew: a team of four including myself went to the back of the appliance to pull off the big 13.5-metre ladder. I was on the left of the ladder below the window. It went up but as it neared the window I had nowhere to put the prop (a metal arm on the ladder providing support). There was a wall to my left stopping me from putting the prop on the ground. I first needed to push the ladder away from the building, but with three others pushing it towards the building I was struggling. Everyone was shouting and the pressure was on. Finally, after what seemed like a lifetime but was only seconds, I pushed the ladder away from the building and moved the prop right and underneath the ladder, making it less than straight but still climbable. Fergal was up the ladder like a whippet (albeit a very large whippet!) and scooped the children from the window like teddy bears from a bedroom shelf.

A B.A. team was upstairs so I went inside with the station officer to firefight and search for casualties on the ground floor. With a hose reel I began fighting the fire in the kitchen while Gordon checked the other downstairs rooms for casualties. He called for assistance and together we carried an unconscious male from the house before going back in to attack the fire in the kitchen. There were six people in total at the house and we rescued four, with the other two making their own way out of the back door. What a relief to radio back to controls: 'All persons accounted for'. The ladder looked as crooked as a dog's hind leg and the boys and I looked back at the incident, laughing at my 'flapping' with the ladder. But our work had been done: a family had been *snatched from the fire*.

* * *

Rewind to my late teens and pre-firefighting days . . . Life was good. I was in my final year studying for an HNC in electronic engineering. I had a wonderful girlfriend who I had been dating for over two years and a great bunch of friends. My studies were 'day release' from work except that I didn't work. It wasn't for lack of trying but it was a difficult time to find a job. My daily routine was generally strict: I got up in the morning before 9 am, had my breakfast which consisted of three or four eggs and cereal, walked to the shop for the newspaper, read the paper with a coffee, and had an early lunch of pasta and tuna before going to the gym for my workout. After training I would eat the rest of my pasta and tuna in the dressing room before relaxing in the sauna/jacuzzi area for an hour. Then home about 3 pm, where I would job hunt or work around the house. Evenings were spent out with my mates and every other weekend was spent with my girlfriend. Like I said, life was good.

On Thursday night the best club in town was Tokyo Joe's, and Jason and I would bus into town for about 9.30 pm and then taxi home. Tokyo Joe's was one of the first dedicated rave clubs in Belfast and it opened only on Thursday nights. I remember how guys used to park their cars there and the boots would be filled with drugs. The police didn't seem to have a clue, or maybe they were too busy chasing terrorists. Inside you danced for hours, sweating like a pig. This wasn't a place to sit on a bar stool, drink beer and chat up the ladies – this was a serious dance venue. I remember making my way home some winter nights shivering with the cold, my sweat-soaked T-shirt stuck to my skin. Saturday nights, if my wallet wasn't empty, were spent mostly at the Egg or the Bot, two night clubs opposite each other in Belfast. We knew loads of people who would hang out there at the weekends: just for a few drinks and a laugh with the mates, nothing more.

I wasn't looking for God but it felt like God was looking for me. It was as if he was on my case, following me and watching me. I would talk about God with my mates after a few drinks and would say to my girlfriend that we should start going to church. I would feel guilty about my wrongs. I was eighteen years of age and felt like I needed rescuing. I was now at the legal age to have a drink and go to clubs but was already becoming a little bored with it. One night we were queuing up to get into a club called Paradise Lost (the new place to go as you had to be over twenty-one to get in!) and I looked at the plaque on the wall outside. It read: 'Paradise Lost – Dedicated to the pursuit of pleasure'. What a message! I was attracted to the clever strapline and began to make it a little motto for my life. I recall writing my name in graffiti and underneath it signing off: 'Dedicated to the pursuit of pleasure.' That motto would come to sum up my attitude to life: chasing the next big fix. I liked that approach, and why not? Isn't the pursuit of pleasure the primary objective in life?

Soon, however, it seemed that the name of the night club and its strapline began to preach at me, as if to say, 'If your only aim is to pursue the pleasures of this life and if all you are dedicated to is chasing after the next quick fix to keep you happy, then paradise will be lost. You will never see it.' God was on my case. Imagine, someone had come up with that name and title and spent money mounting it on the wall in stone all in an attempt to draw people in, but it was drawing me away! God wasn't using a tract or Bible verse to get my attention; he was speaking to me through the very night clubs I was hiding in. I began to ask myself the same question over and over again: surely there must be more to life than this?

I knew I needed to change, but how? I wasn't entirely happy being me – I wanted to be somebody else, somebody better. It wasn't like I suffered from low self-esteem or anything. I happened to like myself a lot, even too much, posing in the gym and shaving my chest. But we all want to be better: better husbands, fathers, friends and people, but change is never easy. I wanted to change some things, fix some things, but not everything. I wanted to set out the terms and conditions of the change: I wasn't attracted to much of the Christianity that I had seen. Gandhi once said, 'I like your Christ. I do not like your Christians. Your Christians are nothing like your Christ.' I agreed with that. I didn't want the Sunday grey-suit thing or to spend my Saturday nights at church as a youth club leader. I pitied those guys and felt that they only took the role because they couldn't be liberated to go and enjoy themselves in the nightclub. Could I be a Christian and not go to church, still get drunk, tell rude jokes and use swear words? I knew the answer was 'no'. My own common sense was plugged in enough to tell me that. I knew I needed to change but I didn't want Jesus to quarantine me. To lose my friends and social life and be put in a sterilized subculture was not for me.

To admit your failures and change direction completely is difficult and I decided I wasn't ready for that. Much as I recognized my faults and was aware that Jesus might have some answers, there were too many questions, too many demands and I didn't want that. Apart from my family, 'Arthur the gardener' was the only friend I had who was a Christian and sometimes we chatted about Christian things over a beer. He wasn't perhaps intellectually the best person to question about Jesus but that suited me. He would just listen without trying to dazzle me with scriptures, which would probably have put me off in any case. He just did what he does best: listened, nodded and smiled. Most of the time I think I answered my own questions.

Months went by and the challenge of change seemed to be written at the bottom of every beer glass. Then out of the blue a guy whom I was friendly with became a Christian. I hadn't seen Thompo (now Pastor Stephen Thompson) for a while and expressed surprise when I heard the news. 'Won't last long,' I said to my friends. 'He's probably going through a wee phase of guilt or being brainwashed by a new girlfriend.' In September I met up with him at a local snooker and golf centre and I remember shaking his hand and saying that I had heard that he had turned 'good living'. As we chatted I closed the conversation by saying that he should invite me to his church some time. It was just small talk and I hoped he wouldn't follow up my pleasantry. He didn't. Now *that* began to bother me a bit. Why didn't he invite me to his church? Was I not good enough?

Would I embarrass him? Maybe God had stopped 'knocking on the door of my heart'?

In October I saw Thompo again. This time we were in two cars belonging to friends that had pulled up at the traffic lights. We wound down the windows (remember the days of winding down windows?) and had a quick 'where-are-you-going, what-are-you-up-to' chat before the lights changed to green. As they did, I said the same thing to him, 'Hey, Thompo, don't forget to invite me to that church of yours!' What was I saying? God must have been on my case.

Two days later the phone rang and by the weekend I was sitting in his church, the Pentecostal church I mentioned earlier with the tambourines. I couldn't wait for the service to end: it was very old-fashioned and although there was much enthusiasm it felt long. But after the service Thompo introduced me to some very friendly people in the church and youth fellowship. There were only about seven at the youth fellowship and it was a very informal night where people seemed happy to chat and get to know one another. That night I saw something in Thompo, Dave and the others I met. They had a sparkle that I didn't have – perhaps they had the missing piece of a jigsaw that I was searching for? In my pursuit of pleasure it seemed I was looking in all the wrong places. Could this be what I was looking for after all?

I returned home and pondered over all the experiences of the night. These people had something that I wanted . . . but I wasn't ready. There was too much at stake and I wasn't prepared just to give this 'Jesus thing' a go for a week or two for I knew this was for life. This was more than another piece in the jigsaw of my life; this was putting the old jigsaw back in the box and starting a new one! No, I wasn't ready, and even if I *was* ready I didn't know what to do next! This was a step of *faith*, and I didn't know if I had enough of that stuff.

For the next few weeks I kept in contact with Thompo and Dave, meeting up on occasions to play pool and snooker. They didn't preach at me or put me under any pressure to make decisions and most of the conversation wasn't about Christianity in any case unless I brought it up. I had seen an advertisement for a special youth service in a local church called Albertbridge Congregational. Some of the leaders were concerned about the teenagers in the community and wanted to hold a special week of services aimed at them. My brother Philip, who had just returned from playing professional football at Ipswich Town, was sharing his testimony (story) along with Stephen Baxter, who was then playing for Linfield FC. I admired both these guys immensely and during my short spell at Linfield FC Stephen had often picked me up in his car to take me to training. I thought I would go along to hear them speak and asked Thompo and Dave if they would join me. They were delighted. In fact I am sure they had a little prayer meeting in the car before they picked me up.

On a cold Tuesday evening in 1992 I sat in an unfamiliar setting for an unforgettable night. From the front Philip and Stephen both spoke about how Jesus was making a difference in their lives and how faith and not football was their priority. After they shared, Roger Carswell came forward to speak about Jesus, and, more importantly for me, how I could become a Christian. I knew I needed to but I wasn't sure how to go about it. If I said 'yes' to Jesus, what were the conditions on the contract? What would be the cost? And what if I failed? I was afraid of failure, that I would 'become' a Christian and end up drunk a few days later.

As I left the church that evening, one of the youth leaders gave me a little booklet called *Journey into Life* by Norman Warren. I had made up my mind: this was what I wanted, and more importantly what I needed, to become a Christian.

That evening I got into bed, turned on the bedside light and held the little booklet in my hands, taking a few minutes to stare at the front cover: a picture of a signpost and an arrow showing the way ahead. This was to be my turning point. It must have looked like a scene from *The Lord of the Rings*, just before Frodo Baggins puts on the ring! What was I expecting: Gandalf? I opened the booklet and read it through. It was very simple with pictures. It highlighted much of what Roger had said that evening. Towards the end there was a little prayer indicating that if I prayed this prayer sincerely then Jesus would come into my life and be my Lord. I paused. Did I have faith in this? Did Jesus make sense to me? I didn't have all the answers but I knew enough. I wanted to pray the prayer but how could I read the prayer and pray? Didn't I have to close my eyes to pray? In Thompo's church lots of people prayed out aloud. Did I have to do that? I am sure God was laughing: even now I felt there was something in my performance that would make it all work! In the end I read the prayer a few times over, memorized it as best I could and closed my eyes and whispered it to God. Nothing happened, at least nothing outward. But there was something inside me that confirmed that this made sense and I had found what I was looking for.

The following morning I took stock of my decision. I needed to take another important step in the process. Stopping now was not an option, for that prayer had set the wheels in motion. I needed to tell someone and there was nobody better than Thompo and Dave. Once I went public and 'out of the closet', so to speak, I felt that I belonged to something new, something exciting and that this was where I belonged, an adopted child in the family of God. I felt like the slate was clean. Jesus had lifted from me all my regrets, my 'bullseye god', shame, anger, fear, insecurities and selfishness and nailed them to the cross. He had taken my messed-up jigsaw in which I was the main character and binned it. There was now a canvas before me, not a jigsaw. It wasn't finished but at the centre it contained a beautiful picture: a skilful artist had painted a masterpiece where Jesus, not me, was centre stage.

In the coming weeks word spread that Mitch had 'got religion'. I was confident about telling friends and surprised that most of them seemed happy for me and supportive. I was also relieved to learn that Jesus had no intention of putting me in an incubator away from any 'contaminants' and so I still made time for the same friends. I would also learn some hard lessons: that bad habits don't die easily and some environments are best avoided. God had been on my case. I believe he snatched me from the fire just at the right time. Another day rejecting his call, pushing away the rescuer, could have cost me dearly.

Nearly two decades have gone by since those early steps as a Christian. There have been many adventures with high points and low points, but never once, *never once* have I regretted the decision I made to follow Jesus. Since I handed him the keys to my life I have had a blast. He is more real to me than ever before, more loving and gracious than I ever imagined, and the canvas isn't finished yet. Life is good. Life is very, very good.

* * *

I used to be a fitness instructor and found a lot of pleasure in that: instructing people how to get fit. Chris, Matt, Roisin and I ran a good gym together. Chris was the manager and looking back was probably the best manager I have ever had in any job. He was enthusiastic, supportive and consistent in his approach and left you to manage the place in his absence, totally confident in your ability. Each client who joined had a fitness assessment, a tailored programme designed to meet their needs, a fitness target to aim for and regular reviews on their progress with updates as necessary. People joined because they wanted to get fit but most had all the wrong ideas about how that would happen. Some thought they needed to train to their maximum everyday; others didn't want to lift weights in case they turned into Arnold Schwarzenegger. It was a learning process for many.

Maybe you're like some of my old gym clients – you want to become a Christian, you know you need to, but you're not sure how to. Maybe you have lots of wrong ideas, fears and misconceptions and are assuming that you need to sign up to a list of do's and don'ts.

Let me give you an induction into the Lord's gym, five simple steps that I want to encourage you to take:

1. Ask for help

   People sometimes arrive at a gym and end up by injuring themselves because they never asked for help. Asking for help is never easy, especially for a man. But we cannot fix the issue of sin by ourselves. You can spend a lifetime under the bonnet of your life trying to fix the engine with a squeezy bottle and some Sellotape but it's not going to work – you need help from a mechanic. The message of Christianity is that we are separated from God by our own selfishness, also called 'sin', and he is the only one who can help us. (I think sin has an I in the middle for a reason!) We have all gone down the Frank Sinatra path singing 'I did it my way' and we need to realize we are lost, that we have been on the wrong path. We're climbing the ladder to put a fire out only to realize the ladder is propped against the wrong building! We cannot know God personally or experience his love and power until we first ask for help.

2. Say sorry

   That's a killer! Recently I had an argument with my wife at dinner time. We don't argue very often but on this occasion I had raised my voice a little. That night I attended a meeting and the issue troubled me. I knew I needed to say sorry, for I had behaved like an idiot. But 'sorry' isn't an easy word to say, so I sent it to her in a text message – what a cop-out!

Difficult as it is to say sorry, it's important for us to get out of the predicament we are in. We need to say sorry to God for the wrong we have committed in our lives. He doesn't expect us to remember every mistake we have made, every harsh word spoken and every need we have neglected, but perhaps as well as a general sorry there are a few specifics we need to ask God to forgive us for.

3. Thank God

There is a saying in the gym, 'No pain, no gain' – meaning that we need to work hard in order to gain maximum benefit from training. But the message on the wall of the 'Lord's gym' could read like this: 'His pain, your gain'.

We need to thank God that through his Son he took the punishment you and I deserved by dying on the cross for our sin. The wages of sin is eternal separation from God: hell. But we no longer need to earn this wage because by dying in our place Jesus took our hell and gave us the gift of eternal life.

4. Invite Jesus to be our personal Lord and Saviour

You can have a year's free pass to the local gym but it will not benefit you personally unless you show up! Jesus is not asking you to become a monk and live in some weird sect. He is simply asking that you believe in him and invite him to take control of your life, to be your steering wheel and not just a spare tyre to use in an emergency. Because God raised Jesus from the dead he is alive and not some abstract god looking at you from afar. He is a personal Saviour. Bernhard Langer, professional golfer and twice US Masters champion, said this, 'After understanding that God loved me so much that He sent His only Son to die for my sins, it was natural to ask the Lord into my life.'[1]

Jesus is the only way to God. He said, 'I am the way and the truth and the life. No-one comes to the Father except through me' (John 14:6). By inviting him to be your Lord and Saviour you are acknowledging that Jesus will rule supremely in your life and that his way will be the way you will strive to follow.

5. Ask God to fill you with his Holy Spirit

God is not natural, but supernatural. God is Spirit and he reveals himself to us by the work of his Holy Spirit. He is not a spook and this point is nothing to do with spooky stuff from a paranormal TV show. God wants to fill us with his Holy Spirit. When Jesus rose from the dead he gave a promise to every believer that they might be filled with power through his Holy Spirit. Jesus does not want us to become members of a dead religion but members of a living Spirit-filled community called the church.

Maybe you are not sure if you are a Christian. Maybe you go to church, you have been baptized and even take the bread and wine to remember Jesus, but you don't know him personally. You are religious but not sure if you have really made a new start with Jesus. You can do this right now.

Lots of people go to church and pretend to be Christians, but why pretend when you can be a real one? Many people go to church just to be seen to do the nice family thing or to impress others. But these motives will never impress God. You may be a member on paper but not in principle. A title or role in a church is not a ticket to heaven. You can be a member of the parish but you can still perish. Today you could change that for ever.

I wonder if you have ever fallen out of love? It can be a sad and painful experience that can fill a person with guilt and regrets. I have a good friend who has fallen out of love with Jesus. He has his eye on someone else now, or should I say some*thing* else: money, career, popularity, family have all wooed him away from his first love. It didn't happen overnight, just gradually, and as the feelings of guilt crashed like waves over his soul he shut himself away from God. Guilt is the most crippling disease in the world today. Psychiatrists and doctors say that unresolved guilt is the number-one cause of mental illness and suicide. But you don't have to live with it because Jesus has never stopped loving you, never given up on you. You may have given up on him but he has never left you.

Becoming a Christian is a step of faith but not a blind leap of faith. As teenagers my friends and I would walk up the local glen and make ourselves a swing from a piece of rope and a stick. We would tie this to the branch of a tree, put the branch between our legs and swing out some twenty feet above the river. It was a leap of faith but not a blind leap for I had checked the knot, put my weight on the branch first and when I was confident that the swing was safe had pushed off from the bank. Every day we take steps of faith: that our car is safe to drive, that the bus driver will take us to the right destination, that the chair we are sitting on will not collapse. Christianity is not blind faith but based on substance. Perhaps the greatest faith that I have ever met is that of the atheist – for they have faith that God does not exist, based on nothing!

You may be ninety years old or in the last stages of terminal cancer, but it's never too late. You could be reading this in prison or in your bedroom, but the venue doesn't matter either. The Bible says, 'Today, if you hear his voice, do not harden your hearts' and 'Now is the time of God's favour, now is the time of salvation' (Hebrews 3:15; 2 Corinthians 6:2). My book is intended to give you one answer to all your questions and that answer is Jesus. I don't know of one predicament that you will find yourself in where Jesus does not have answers. He is the way, he is the truth and he is the life. He wants to be your Lord and Saviour, to snatch you from the fire and save you. To give you a hope, a purpose and a destiny, to take your hell and give you heaven, to turn your mourning into dancing.

Here is a prayer that you can pray as a way of starting the Christian life. Just read these words as if they were your personal letter to God:

Dear Father,
Thank you for sending your Son, Jesus, to die for me on
    the cross.
I am truly sorry for the wrong things I have done in my life.
Forgive me my sins as I now turn away from everything I know
    to be wrong.
I now invite you to come into my life as my personal Saviour
    and Lord.
Fill me with your Holy Spirit and help me to live for you.
Through Jesus Christ I pray this prayer,
Amen.

By praying this prayer you have made a life-changing step. The Bible says, 'If you confess with your mouth, "Jesus is Lord," and believe in your heart that God raised him from the dead, you will be saved' (Romans 10:9).

If you know another Christian, go and tell them you have prayed this prayer and that you are now a follower of Jesus. They can help you in the next part of the journey and encourage you in your faith. I know this may not be an easy step for many reasons, but it is important to share your decision with others.

But whether or not you know another Christian, keep reading for the journey is just starting . . .

10. Girls' legs:
Equipped for the journey

In the summer of 2006 I was travelling with the family to France for a well-deserved holiday. We have a caravan in the Vendée region and love spending a few weeks there in the summer, chilling out with a good book and excellent food and attending some of the Bible studies at Spring Harvest. On this occasion we decided to travel by car, driving down through the Republic of Ireland before boarding the overnight ferry to France. While Amanda took her turn at driving and baby Noah slept, I started reading *Long Way Round* by Ewan McGregor and Charlie Boorman, a brilliant book and television series following two actors on their crazy challenge of riding around the world on BMW motorbikes. I began daydreaming mid-chapter, longing for a new challenge for myself. I was at that time without a motorbike so a world tour was out of the question, but what about a cycle? I looked at the map of Ireland for an idea. Could I cycle from the bottom to the top, from the most southerly to the most northerly point? At home I had a mountain bike but the farthest I had travelled was only twenty-five miles. Would I be able to ride 420 miles, the whole length of Ireland? How long would it take? My mind began to work on a plan: five days would be the target and I would raise money for charity. I shared my thoughts with Amanda and she gave a sympathetic nod to my scheme. (My poor wife has to put up with my wild ideas but thankfully is very supportive.) Now I would need some advice from a cyclist, but who did I know who was experienced enough to advise me? There was a fire officer in Central Fire Station in Belfast. I had never spoken to him personally but I knew he was a keen cyclist. His name was Harry Dawson.

We soon boarded the ferry and once we had unpacked our overnight bag we went for a look around the boat. It wasn't long before I recognized a face coming my way that did more than send a shiver down my spine. It was Harry Dawson. Harry and his wife, Thea, were on their way to France for two weeks and had just happened to book the same ferry times as us, travelling to and from France! As he was walking past I stopped to introduce myself and we chatted briefly before I told him my thoughts about a cycle from the bottom to the top of Ireland. 'Malin Head to Mizen Head. I have done that route before,' he said. I couldn't believe it – the coincidence was scary! We agreed to meet up after the holidays to discuss the idea further.

Harry and I met in my office and he gave me a brief on the challenge. He went straight to the point – there are no back doors with him. First, I wasn't going to do the trip on a mountain bike; that would be needless suffering. I needed a road-racing-style bike. I would need a support team to carry provisions such as food. And the challenge would take a winter of training with the target for late spring. The route was best attacked from south to north as the Met Office said typical winds at that time of year were southerly, allowing the wind to be on my back rather than in my face. Finally Harry said, 'You're not going to do this alone. I will ride with you and train with you over the winter for the challenge.'

I was delighted by his support and advice and soon managed to receive sponsorship for a new bike and clothing. In January we started training. For five months we went out two or three times a week building up my stamina and bike skills as Harry pushed me hard. I had run marathons before and trained at various levels for football and charity challenges but this was different. On the first day we covered over thirty miles and I was shattered. We stopped at Harry's house and he took me in for a cup of tea and toast before allowing me to cycle home –

I needed the sustenance! He laughed, calling me 'a big Nancy', and the name has stuck ever since.

By May I was cycling the Ards Peninsula alone, covering the seventy-four miles in under four hours. I was much stronger now but could I get on the bike and cover the same distance day after day? Trevor 'Bunter' Brown was enlisted to drive a support vehicle with a spare bike kit and food for the trip. Bunter is a firefighter on my watch who joined the same year as Harry, in 1980. They were good friends and I could tell there would be plenty of Northern Ireland banter on the trip.

On 10 June we travelled down to our start point of Mizen Head. Puffy white clouds hung in a beautiful blue sky, and while sipping tea during a short stop for lunch everyone commented that conditions were perfect. I had read in a magazine that Mizen Head held the record for the least amount of rain in Ireland and I shared this with the team. They rolled their eyes, suggesting that this was the worst thing to say. True enough, at 5 am as I lay in bed near our start point, the rain bounced off the Velux window above me. It rained every day of the challenge, and as for the Met Office reports of southerly winds, they were in my face the whole time!

We set off early wearing waterproofs as raindrops danced on potholed rural roads. I came off my bike after only ten miles and nursed cuts to my knee, elbow, hands and hip as well as a sore shoulder. I had a puncture in Bantry and the hill climb at Glengarriff took us up above clouds on a difficult two-mile climb in chilly winds. At Kenmare we took a wrong turn on a minor road before riding through Killarney and hammering the last twenty-five miles to Tralee. What a start! The first day was over and I was sore and tired after 102 wet and windy miles.

Harry was much stronger than me and during training I had wondered if he would leave me to suffer alone and ride on to the next stop point. But before we left he said something very spiritual and reassuring: 'Remember I will never leave you.' Every day was a challenge but Harry was true to his word. Once he did ride on ahead of me leaving me to suffer, but only for an hour and it was all part of the fun of the trip.

On that particular day the wind and rain were hard on our faces, roads were hilly and my average speed was down to sixteen mph. Harry and I were both tired and just wanted to get the day over and done with. We arranged for Bunter to meet us in the village of Charlestown for a quick cup of tea before cycling on to that day's finishing point, Dromahair. We pulled up by the side of the road and some of the kids from the local 'travelling community' (gypsies) came over and started teasing us about our lycra clothing and fancy shoes. Harry was in no mood for it, and after constant taunts of 'Girls' legs, girls' legs' I could see he was starting to get very annoyed. Then they started poking at his bike – wrong thing to do – you never touch Harry's bike! He shouted so they poked it some more before he finally threw the rest of his tea over one of them. (Don't worry, it wasn't hot!) The kid went mad saying the kind of words I had shared with my dentist, before kicking Harry's bike. Harry decided enough was enough and it was time to get on the bikes and ride on. That was when I suggested that Bunter should take a photo of me with the kids as a souvenir. I thought it was all a bit funny. Harry lost it. Off he went up the road with me cycling behind him like a child. We laughed later but he declined to take a copy of the photo as a memento of the trip!

We finally completed the Mizen to Malin challenge in an appalling downpour of rain. Some friends joined us for the last day, a swansong home, but even with 'fresh legs' they suffered more than Harry or me. Over the trip we had some close shaves. On the road to Milltown a lorry blew a steel road sign into the air. It went over my head and under Harry's wheel. Had it hit us we would have suffered serious injuries. In the Blue Stack

Mountains we were both hit by bottles thrown from a passing van, and a car clipped my elbow on another stretch of road. Official Met Office reports stated this was the worst June on record, but we made it. I am grateful to Harry and Bunter for their support. The journey was never meant to be done alone.

* * *

In another sense we are all on a journey. In fact we are travelling in more ways than we perhaps realize. As I write this book in Belfast, I am moving at 620 miles per hour due to the rotation of the earth's axis. (Depending on where you are reading the book the measurement will be different.) That's enough to make me hold on to my coffee a little tighter! But it gets better: the earth is also travelling around the sun at 10,000 miles per hour – dizzy yet? I think I need to go and lie down!

Then there is the journey of life – living in the dash, as I call it. Go to my parents' grave and you will see these words on a headstone:

Our very special Mum and Dad
Gerry 30/12/1932 – 6/2/1987
Marion 13/7/1939 – 10/7/1999
'I have fought the good fight, I have finished the race,
I have kept the faith' 2 Timothy 4:7

That little scripture is an attempt to sum up life in the dash for my parents. All of us are living between two significant dates: our birth and our death. What happens in between is the journey of life. Some of us may be a little closer to one date than the other, but one thing is for sure: we are all on the journey of life and there will be no rerun or second chance.

There is a headstone beside my parents' which has a name, two dates with a dash in between them and that's it. No comment, no thought or scripture, nothing. Just a tiny dash: a negative or a minus sign. I have often wondered what life's purpose was for that person. Of course a headstone message does not give a full picture of a person's life but it does seem to ask a question: in this amazing journey, what will that life amount to?

Charlie Murray, whom we met in the Introduction, is 102 years old and attends my church. He is an amazing man who became a Christian at just thirteen years of age. Recently I interviewed him for a magazine, and as we talked I became very aware that life moves very fast and we need to make it count: every step, every thought, every heartbeat. King Solomon once wrote: 'There is a way that seems right to a person, but in the end it leads to death' (Proverbs 14:12). I am sure you have all heard the saying: 'It seemed like a good idea at the time!' But let's not spend our life going along wrong paths. The journey is yours to travel. You can determine much of the route: whom you travel with, what baggage you bring and when to rest, among other things. But one thing is for sure – you are not intended to travel alone.

For those of us who have become Christians a new journey has begun – a journey towards heaven. This journey can be rewarding and very exciting, but also difficult with many hazards along the way as we spend time in the valleys as well as on the mountain tops.

In 1678 John Bunyan published the first part of his allegorical book *The Pilgrim's Progress*, a fantastic story sharing the highs and lows of the Christian journey. The name of each person that 'Christian' meets on the journey reveals their character. Every place on the journey has a name revealing its characteristics too. Christian meets Evangelist (not the money-grabbing TV sort!), Help, Goodwill, Faithful and Hopeful, as well as Hypocrisy, Envy, Superstition, Ignorance and Atheist. He travels through the Valley of Humiliation and enters Doubting Castle, among many other locations, before finally reaching the Celestial City. Having been written over 230 years ago, the writing style is, as you can imagine, very old-fashioned and not easy to read. However, it offers a classic picture of the challenges every Christian faces and is as relevant today as when it was first written. John Bunyan wrote the story to encourage and help equip Christians.

* * *

I recently competed in a triathlon-style race which involved cycling off road on a mountain bike, climbing a mountain and canoeing across a lake. I was captain of a team and we travelled to Penrith in the English Lake District to compete in a charity event called Race the Sun. The night before the race we sat together in a sports hall with the sixty-six other teams, and I started to get a little anxious about the challenge before us. As the race marshal began to brief the teams, things were looking a little bit more challenging than we had first anticipated. Was the marshal exaggerating? Or was this going to be a brutal day's work? We decided to take his advice and were very glad we did! His advice included the following: work as a team, avoid the bog (i.e. do not attempt to cycle through it), prepare for bad weather, communicate clearly with officials at checkpoints, use a map, follow obvious signposts, check equipment, eat and drink plenty, and endeavour to keep team spirits high. All good advice! We finished in seventh place and raised over £2,500 for charity.

During the rest of this chapter I want to play the role of 'race marshal' for your journey as a Christian, not because I am an expert or have completed the course, but because I am keen to help you make not only a good start but a great finish.

Essential kit guide

- The Bible
- Prayer
- The church

The Bible

The Bible is consistently the number-one best-selling book in the world. However, it is more than a book. In fact it is a collection of books written by many different authors over hundreds of years.

Psalm 119:105 says, 'Your word is a lamp to my feet and a light for my path.' The Bible can be a light to lead us through the dark places. I like that idea, for there is no better feeling for a firefighter who has been working in smoke and darkness than to see the light of a torch. The Bible gives us direction, reassurance and encouragement and is essential for our all-round spiritual growth and maturity. The Bible has been described as a love letter from God, a manual for life and a map for the journey, but none of these metaphors can really do it justice! There is no other book quite like it and therefore nothing to measure it against.

The main theme of the Bible is God's relationship with the human race. It answers the questions:

- Who are we?
- Where did we come from?
- Why are we here?
- Where are we going?
- How should we live?

The Bible is the Word of God, written by various authors but behind each of them one author: the Spirit of God. That is what makes it special, for it is God-breathed, God-inspired and therefore a living book.

Above all other books that a Christian should ever read, this has to be the priority. But how should we read it? If you have never read it, or you started reading it once but got fed up, let me encourage you to discover it afresh. There are several ways to begin, but strange as it may seem I do not suggest that you just start at Genesis and attempt to read from start to finish. Below are three options:

- Use Bible-reading notes. There are some excellent reading notes to help you get started.[1]
- Choose a book from the Bible and read it through. I suggest that if you are a new Christian you start by reading one of the accounts of Jesus' life in the Gospels. Start by reading Luke's Gospel, a chapter a day, and think about what Jesus is saying to you through the passage. Don't be afraid to highlight any verses that stand out for you.
- Choose a character or key word in the Bible and do a study on it. Many Bibles have a concordance at the back, and often people find it helpful to look up a key word such as 'love' and study what the Bible has to say about it. You could also follow the life of a character such as Joseph or Daniel.

In addition to the above, it is important that you learn the Bible from others: in church, Bible studies or small groups. God gives some people a special gifting to teach and help you understand his book. Listen to what the pastor or Bible teacher says and don't be afraid to ask questions.

If you don't have a copy of the Bible and can't afford one, don't be afraid to ask a local church for a copy. If you still have no success, then please contact my office and we will send you a New Testament free of charge![2] Please read the Bible for yourself with an open heart and mind. Ask God to speak to you personally though its message, and he will.

When faced with one of the most intense challenges of his life, evangelist Billy Graham knelt down with his Bible and began to pray something like this: 'O Lord, there are many things in this book I don't understand . . . but Father, by faith I am going to accept this as your Word. From this moment on, I am going to read and trust the Bible as the Word of God.'

That prayer became a turning point in Billy Graham's journey.

Prayer

What is prayer? I was brought up with the understanding that it was talking to God. But it's much more than that. It's best described as communicating with God, with talking being only part of the process. Prayer is also about listening to God. In fact the older I get, the more I find myself listening to God more than talking to him. But there is another element to prayer which is much deeper and more beautiful than this. It's hard to describe, but it's like when I am alone and I walk among the orange of autumn and the river talks to me and I feel alive, powerful and free, or when I hold my son or daughter on my knee and we don't need to say anything. It's when I walk outside on a spring morning and I lift my face towards the sun like a little meerkat and feel the warmth of its rays on my face for the first time after a cold winter. I wish I could describe prayer to you, but it is indescribable for me.

Tony Campolo put it like this:

There is a kind of praying where you ask nothing, you hear nothing, you just surrender, and the Spirit of the living Christ, the Christ who died on Calvary invades you and possesses you and transforms you from within. That's what gives hope and that's what creates faith – the Spirit of God creates faith. The Holy Spirit creates faith. Jesus entering into us creates faith.[3]

In Matthew 6:5–18 Jesus teaches us about prayer. The early church devoted themselves to prayer (Acts 2:42–47) and we would do well to do the same. Below are some helpful points to get you started:

- Find a quiet place free from distraction. That is not always easy. I often find the best time is early in the morning before the rest of the family are up.
- Be honest. Share with God from your heart. He is not looking for fancy words or a ritual of vain repetitions.
- Ask God's Holy Spirit to help you to pray. Romans 8:26 says, 'In the same way, the Spirit helps us in our weakness. We do not know what we ought to pray for, but the Spirit himself intercedes for us with groans that words cannot express.'
- Listen to the prayers of others. Not only can we agree with their prayers but learn from godly men and women.
- Pray expectantly. In Mark 11:24 Jesus says, 'Therefore I tell you, whatever you ask for in prayer, believe that you have received it, and it will be yours.'
- Be persistent. Until you hear God saying 'no', keep praying for a 'yes'.
- Keep a record of your prayer requests. Write them in a little prayer diary. You might just be surprised at how many God will answer. This can be a great source of encouragement and motivation.

The highlights of my prayer life have not been the long lists of answered prayers or miracles I have seen, although they have been there. The highlights have been how prayer has deepened my relationship with God, increased my sensitivity to the Holy Spirit and at times flooded my life with compassion for others. My prayer life keeps me focused on the journey.

The church

My wife is a manager in fashion retail and she will tell you that fashion is different for everyone, depending on their individual style. I like John Rocha clothing. John is a tiny man originally from Hong Kong, but now based in Ireland. He looks like a Navaho Indian, only he carries a man-bag instead of a tomahawk. I met him in London recently and he signed my John Rocha T-shirt (I am a sad individual!). John Rocha clothing suits my style; I even have a John Rocha coffee table and his picture frames at home. But you would not catch my brother wearing John Rocha clothing – he wears Paul Smith.

I also like body art. Tattoos can be super trendy, and some evenings I watch *Miami Ink* and love how people express their feelings and their faith through a tattoo. I would love to get a tattoo of my children's names on my wrists written in a Celtic font, but I'm afraid. Not of the pain but of what people will say – what a wimp!

As we travel on the journey of life, it is important that we do not travel alone. In fact, I believe that every Christian should be a member of a local church. The denomination you choose to belong to will often come down to personal choice and style. I love my home church but it's not everyone's preference. We are a trendy church with a busy café serving vanilla lattes and sandwiches filled with brie, caramelized onions, sun-blushed tomatoes and Italian ham. People come in their jeans, our keyboard player wears shorts, and my wife preached last week in her flip-flops! Last Sunday I visited another local church. The men were dressed in their best Sunday suits while the ladies wore hats, and I walked in wearing a flowery John Rocha shirt and sporting stubble. I didn't intend to offend anyone but I think I did. I just wanted to attend somewhere different for one night but it just wasn't my style.

No matter what it looks like, here are seven very important components that every church should have:

- *Good Bible teaching*. The right church for you must be one in which the Bible is opened and taught, and where members are encouraged to read it for themselves. A good Bible-teaching church will teach that faith in Jesus Christ alone is the only way to eternal life.
- *The Holy Spirit*. D. L. Moody said, 'It is easier for a man to breathe without air than it is for a Christian to live without the Holy Spirit.' Nuff said.
- *Worship that enables you to encounter God and express your love for him*. It doesn't need to be loud or modern. It just needs to help you focus on Christ.
- *Friendly people with whom you can celebrate your faith in God and who can help you deepen your relationship with him*. Other believers are your brothers and sisters in Christ and together you should encourage one another. The word for this is 'fellowship'. My friend 'Trevor the joiner' describes fellowship like this: 'Fellowship is when two fellows buy a ship, and do life together on the ship.' I talked in chapter 3 about having good 'defence mechanisms' when it comes to temptation. Good, honest fellowship and support from other men can make a big difference. (My friends Philip and Geoff and I meet once a month for prayer and support. We ask honest questions and give honest answers. I find it a great help.)
- *A heart for non-Christians*. By this I mean a church focused on sharing the love of God with others,

expressed in many ways, including practically helping the poor and needy, visiting and praying for the sick and elderly, as well as making the message of Jesus Christ known in the community.

- *Opportunities to get involved*. God has not given anyone the gift to be just a bum on a pew! Every Christian has a part to play in the family of God.
- *Baptism and communion as signs of a transformed life*.

Being a Christian will bring many challenges and you will feel like a failure sometimes, but don't give up – keep striving to follow Jesus.

Brennan Manning wrote in his book entitled *The Ragamuffin Gospel*:

> Often I have been asked, 'Brennan, how is it possible that you became an alcoholic after you got saved?' It is possible because I got battered and bruised by loneliness and failure, because I got discouraged, uncertain, guilt-ridden, and took my eyes off Jesus. Because the Christ-encounter did not transfigure me into an angel. Because justification by grace through faith means I have been set in right relationship with God, not made the equivalent of a patient etherised on a table.[4]

With that in mind, pack up your kit and let's go . . .

11. Tartan army: Celebrating Jesus

The atmosphere outside the stadium was like a carnival. The crowd was buzzing with anticipation and excitement. The fact that this was one of the first football games to be played in the new 80,000-seater stadium made it special. Added to that, it was the opening game of the 1998 World Cup, and with the mighty Brazil playing it was a mouth-watering prospect. And there was another factor which took the experience to a completely different level: Scotland were Brazil's opponents.

Scotland and Northern Ireland football fans are the best in the world bar none (in my opinion). I am a massive Chelsea fan, and some of their most loyal supporters are from Scotland and Northern Ireland. In fact the best away game you can go to watch Chelsea play is against Sunderland. Why? Because it's near the border and hundreds of Scottish Chelsea fans travel down to the game while Northern Irish Chelsea fans grab cheap flights to Newcastle and then on to Sunderland.

Northern Ireland had failed, once again, to reach the World Cup finals, so the Mitchell family decided to go and watch the other home nations who qualified: Scotland and England. With our William Wallace face paint on, the Mitchell brothers, their WAGS and my little nephew Jamie were soaking up the atmosphere like a sponge. Paris became alive with a sea of blue as over 60,000 Scottish fans dressed in football shirts, tartan scarves, kilts, Jimmy hats and spilt lager danced and sang from the Champs-Elysées to the Stade de France. You could have mistaken the whole occasion for Hogmanay had it not been for the samba drums and blue skies. The Scots had arrived in their thousands, by any means possible: I met a lad who had hitch-hiked from Glasgow, with no ticket for the game and not a penny left in his pocket. That afternoon I also watched a fishing trawler that had departed from Aberdeen travel up the River Seine. It was like *Pirates of the Caribbean*, with men hanging from the sails wearing tricorne hats, eyepatches and swigging rum or Buckfast.

Having climbed the steps of the stadium and entered the arena, the scene was breathtaking. Fans from Brazil and other nations around the world had assembled to see the launch of the greatest sporting event on earth: the World Cup. As both teams warmed up I was in awe of the yellow shirt, sky-blue shorts and white socks of Brazil. As a child playing football in the Belfast streets, I had wanted to be a Brazilian legend in that famous kit – Zico, Pele or Socrates? Now I was about to watch the mighty Brazil live. Scottish fans were relentless in their passion and singing, as this was undoubtedly the biggest stage on which Scotland's national football team had ever performed. After a rousing rendition of 'Flower of Scotland' by players and fans, the match got under way.

Brazil scored an early goal that would have left English fans silent, but not so for the Scottish. The singing continued, and at thirty-seven minutes Scotland was awarded a penalty. The cheers from the fans would have burst a samba drum, never mind an eardrum – welcome to tinnitus island!

John Collins put the ball on the spot and every Scot in the stadium was a bag of nerves. Big hairy homophobic men held hands and stood arm in arm as he stepped back from the ball to take the kick. Collins, cool as a cucumber, slotted the ball into the bottom corner with consummate ease! Goal, goal, goal! There was absolute euphoria as Scotland fans jumped and danced, hugged and kissed. Jimmy Hill could have called it a toe-poke, a mis-kick or a slip, but all of Scotland didn't care. They had scored against the world champions and were back in the game.

* * *

The world needs Christians to be filled with this same passion. Before a mocking world who thought they had no chance against the might of Brazil, those Scots sang their hearts out. Pride, passion and belief were burning in the hearts of thousands. I met whole families who had rearranged their holidays just to be there. People sold possessions to buy tickets and pay for accommodation. Yet some Christians can't even get out of bed for Jesus. If being a Christian is the greatest thing in your life, why keep it a secret? If Jesus has become your own personal Lord and Saviour, why wouldn't you want to share this with others? Why would you not be willing to follow him no matter what the cost? I am amazed that so many people are so unamazed at God's amazing love . . . Some of you need to read that again! Where is our pride, our passion, our belief?

I watch Christians hide their faith during the week and when confronted they tell me it's a 'private faith'. How can you take the command of Jesus to go into all the world and share the gospel (Matthew 28:19–20) and make it private? It's criminal! One person introduced me to a friend saying he was a 'covert' Christian, indicating that he worked undercover for Jesus. That may sound impressive but it's not biblical. Jesus says, 'Let your light shine before men' (Matthew 5:16), not 'put it under a bucket'! To have the cure for sin and hide it is a sin in itself. Indeed, the greatest sin in the church today is not what we do; it's what we *don't* do! The sin of omission, the sin of doing nothing.

I watch men who sit in church on a Sunday as if it were a funeral and Jesus was still in the tomb! They tell me they are 'not given to emotion'. Why is it then that when Ulster scores a try or their football team scores a goal, they jump up and down and cheer? If I can travel to Stamford Bridge and go crazy with excitement and joy when a leather bag of air leaves the grass and goes between two white posts and into a net, is it not normal that I should celebrate Jesus with even more passion? Jesus was beaten all night, lashed with a whip, showered with spit and left spiked to a tree to die, before rising from the dead, offering forgiveness to a dying world. When you believe passionately in something, you talk it up, you make time for it and you invest in it. If you are serious about God, you will be serious about expressing this faith to the world.

I do not believe there is a more pressing challenge to every believer today than the challenge to share Jesus with pride, passion and belief. Compared with sharing Jesus, everything else happening in the church is like rearranging the furniture when the house is on fire! There is nothing more important than fulfilling the call to share Christ with a lost and dying world. The lyrics of that old African-American song urge us:

Go, tell it on the mountain,
Over the hills and far away.
Go tell it on the mountain,
That Jesus Christ is Lord.

God said this to Ezekiel: 'When I say to the wicked, "You will surely die," and you do not warn them or speak out to dissuade them from their evil ways in order to save their lives, those wicked people will die for their sins, and I will hold you account-able for their blood' (Ezekiel 3:18).

Often church leaders ask me: what motivates you to share your faith? How can I get the people out of the pews and into the community to share the love of God?

For me it was (and still is) the most natural thing in the world. I understood the night I became a Christian that I needed to share the gospel with others. In fact, at the end of the little booklet I had read it said this: 'Witness – Tell one other person

within the next 24 hours what you have done – that you sur-
rendered your life to Christ. Don't be ashamed to be known as
a Christian at work and at home.' The next day I told my
Christian friends, the day after that I told my family, and by the
weekend my girlfriend and all my non-Christian friends knew.

For others, sharing Jesus may not be so natural. It may be
generally a little bit more of a challenge or perhaps even a
frightening thought. Don't panic, for Jesus is not asking everyone to go to the city centre with a megaphone, a sandwich
board with Bible verses on it and a duffel bag full of tracts! We
are all called to evangelism, but we are not all called to do it in
a specific way, you will be glad to hear. Evangelism is just a
fancy word for communicating the good news of Jesus.

Here's some advice to help you share your faith with others:

- Be intentional! Evangelism has nothing to do with
  manipulating a crowd, squeezing money from people
  or whipping up a frenzy of emotions. Neither is it about
  dumping information on people or shouting judgment.
  It's a lifestyle.

  Make sharing Jesus part of your lifestyle. People will
  read the book of our lives before they hear the words
  from our lips. We need to see people as God sees them,
  loving them and showing Jesus to them as the Saviour
  of the world. You are possibly the only Christian some of
  your friends or work colleagues know – what a privilege
  to be an ambassador for God. More than 75% of people
  become Christians because of the witness of a friend or
  family member. However, you can hang out with your
  friends all day at the golf course or gym, but unless your
  friendship evangelism is intentional you are missing the
  point! Pray and ask God for opportunities, try to weave
  your faith into the conversation and listen to what others

are saying. Find out their views on Jesus and what stops them from becoming a Christian.

- Focus on your story. No-one can deny your personal experience of Jesus. This makes your story a wonderful tool in your hands. Take time to write it down, breaking it into three sections: life before you were a Christian; how you became a Christian; and what has happened since.

- Overcome your fear! Often people avoid sharing their faith because they are gripped by fear – fear of rejection, failure, appearing hypocritical or losing friends. We all want to be loved and accepted, so it is difficult to introduce something that can become confrontational and offensive.

  First, remember that this fear is normal. I have been doing evangelism for nearly twenty years and still become fearful at times. Paul the apostle was afraid to evangelize. When entering Corinth he was determined to be true to the message of Christ and the cross, but he admitted that he came to them 'in weakness and fear, and with much trembling' (1 Corinthians 2:3). Fear does not mean that you are not up to the task. It's a natural reaction to facing the unknown, and the challenge is not removing fear but overcoming it! The apostles Peter, John and Paul all prayed for boldness in order to proclaim the message of Jesus. Fear will do one of two things: it will either drive us away from evangelism or drive us to our knees in prayer. Prayer and evangelism operate hand in hand, and fear is ironically often a great friend that reminds us that we cannot do the task without God's help.

- Keep your evangelism simple. You don't have to have a degree in theology or have been a Christian for a long time in order to grasp an opportunity. In 2008 Chelsea lost the Champions League final. Captain John Terry had slipped as he took the deciding penalty and missed. He was devastated (and so was I). The next day I was talking to my then two-year-old son, telling him that John Terry was very sad. He suggested we get him a present to cheer him up. I asked what kind of present and he said, 'A book'. That afternoon I sent John Terry a Christian book called *Blue Like Jazz* by Don Miller, and wrote a letter explaining my son's suggestion and reminding him that there are more important things in life than penalties and football. A few months later John Terry wrote a lovely letter back thanking Noah and me for the book and saying how he had appreciated our support.

Now if a two-year-old child can witness to the Chelsea and England captain through a book, what can *you* do for God today?

- Know and share the Bible. Your story of how you became a Christian is very important. Your opinion on things will be valuable, but the Word of God is more powerful still. My late friend Gerald Titmus, to whom this book is dedicated, was a great evangelist. I remember him 'skilling me up' as a young Christian and getting me to memorize just five key scriptures to help me in my witnessing. They were:

  1. Romans 3:23: 'All have sinned and fall short of the glory of God.'
  2. Romans 6:23: 'The wages of sin is death, but the gift of God is eternal life in Christ Jesus our Lord.'
  3. Romans 5:8: 'God demonstrates his own love for us in this: While we were still sinners, Christ died for us.'
  4. Romans 10:9: 'If you confess with your mouth, "Jesus is Lord," and believe in your heart that God raised him from the dead, you will be saved.'

5. John 3:16: 'For God so loved the world that he gave his one and only Son, that whoever believes in him shall not perish but have eternal life.'

He called it 'The Romans Road to heaven' and encouraged me to share this message with others in the following way:

We are all sinners (Romans 3:23), in that our sin deserves punishment (Romans 6:23). The good news of the gospel is that Jesus died in our place, taking the punishment we deserved (Romans 5:8). If we believe in Jesus and confess him as Lord, he will forgive our sins and give us eternal life (Romans 10:9). The final verse (John 3:16) was one you gave to your friend to take away with them. You could write it down to help them remember the message you shared.

I pray that God's Holy Spirit will empower each of us to be intentional in our evangelism, overcome our fear, read our Bibles and tell the world that Jesus lives.

Over the last ten years it has been a joy to work with a dedicated team at Crown Jesus Ministries in communicating the good news of Jesus. We want people to crown Jesus Lord of their lives, put him first and give him pre-eminence over everything they think, say and do.

It is our desire that one day everyone will stand before Jesus in heaven and cast their crowns at his feet, as a symbol of their love and commitment to him.

Make sure you have something of value to cast at Jesus' feet on that day.

Jude verse 23 says, 'Snatch others from the fire and save them.' This is the motto of Fire Fighters for Christ International. It's also my motto in life. Make it yours too!

Notes

1. Dracula: The problem is me

1. C. S. Lewis, *Surprised by Joy* (Fontana, 1955).

2. Lemon and Peartree Hill: Broken world

1. John Blanchard, *Where is God When Things Go Wrong?* (Evangelical Press, 2005), pp. 8–12.
2. Ibid.
3. Ibid.
4. Statistics taken from *The Lancet* (Child survival series, 2003).
5. W. Tullian Tchividjian, quoting Winston Churchill, in his article, 'Getting to the Heart of the Problem' (www.banneroftruth.org/pages/articles/article_detail.php?966).
6. C. S. Lewis, *The Problem of Pain* (HarperCollins, 2002; first published 1940).

3. Sex: Who decides what is right and wrong?

1. Quote by popular Scottish poet and essayist Alexander Smith (1830–1867).
2. Quoted in David Knox and Caroline Schacht, *Choices in Relationships: An Introduction to Marriage and the Family* (Wadsworth Publishing, 2007).
3. From survey entitled 'The Invisible Generation', quoted by Nick Pollard, *Evangelism Made Slightly Less Difficult* (IVP, 1997), p. 62.
4. C. S. Lewis, *Mere Christianity* (HarperCollins, 2002), p. 31.

4. A box of chocolates: Loving church

1. Quoted by Greg Haslam (www.thissideofthecross.com).
2. Quoting from their song, 'Everything's Gonna Be Alright'.
3. Stephen Gaukroger, *It Makes Sense* (Scripture Union, 1998), p. 122.

4. Billy Graham, *Just As I Am* (HarperCollins, 1997), p. 160.
5. From the song 'U Can't Go 2 Church' written by Keith Lancaster, copyright 1990 Anthony K. Music. Used by permission.
6. Statistics taken from Rick Warren's Global P.E.A.C.E. Plan Conference 2004 (see www.thepeaceplan.com) and Malaria No More, a member of Malaria Consortium (www.malarianomore.org).

5. Knocking on the door: Hearing the right message
1. Ranulph Fiennes, *Mad, Bad and Dangerous to Know* (Hodder & Stoughton, 2007), p. 170.
2. See Revelation 3:20.
3. Quotation taken from Wanda Vassallo, *Speaking with Spirit* (Ambassador Publications, 2005).
4. Lynne Truss, *Eats Shoots and Leaves: The Zero Tolerance Approach to Punctuation* (Profile Books, 2003) p. 9.

6. Coffee: *The Passion of the Christ*
1. National Basketball Association.
2. Josephus, *Antiquities* XVIII 63f.
3. Tacitus, *Annals* 15:44.
4. *The Letters of Pliny the Younger*, Book 10.
5. Eusebius of Caesarea, *Church History*.

7. Arthur the gardener: God's amazing grace
1. Find this account in Donald McCullagh, *Say Please, Say Thank you: The Respect We Owe One Another* (Putnam, 1999).
2. Max Lucado, *In the Grip of Grace* (Word Publishing, 1996), p. 71.

8. Alive: Exploding some myths
1. Bill Bryson, *A Short History of Nearly Everything* (Black Swan, 2004), p. 17.
2. Details taken from Josh McDowell, 'Evidence for the Resurrection' (www.josh.org).

3. Quoted in Lee Strobel, *The Case for Faith* (Zondervan, 2000), pp. 199–200.
4. Quoting from Michael Green, *Man Alive* (IVP, 1968).
5. Taken from Ross Clifford, *The Case for the Empty Tomb* (Albatross Books, 1993).

9. Snatched from the fire: The Lord's gym
1. Bernhard Langer, *My Autobiography* (Hodder & Stoughton, 2002), p. 50.

10. Girls' legs: Equipped for the journey
1. Reading notes include: *Every Day with Jesus for New Christians* by Selwyn Hughes; *The Word for Today* by Bob Gass (free copies available from UCB); and *Life with Lucas* by Jeff Lucas. These reading notes use the experience of other Christians to help you get the best from the text.
2. Contact info@crownjesus.org
3. Tony Campolo, 'It's Friday, But Sunday's Coming' (PDF file available at www.tonycampolo.org).
4. Brennan Manning, *The Ragamuffin Gospel* (Authentic, 2007), p. 14.

Mitch is part of a wonderful team of evangelists and staff working with Crown Jesus Ministries in Ireland. Their mission statement is 'to see the people of Ireland crown Jesus Lord of their lives'.

Crown Jesus Ministries are committed to communicating the Good News of Jesus in a clear and relevant way. Their work reaches a broad spectrum of people and incorporates the following:

Klass Kids: A puppet and children's ministry running after-schools clubs, assemblies and church services.

One Way and **HUB**: Two powerful outreach and training programmes for teenagers and young adults.

'If my people . . . ': An initiative calling the nation to prayer. This includes prayer events and training in prayer ministry.

Alive Events: These adult-based programmes include: an evangelism training course, joint church outreach, a five-week course exploring the message of Jesus, as well as many other outreach opportunities and events.

Partner Church Projects: These projects exist to support, motivate and release the local church to do outreach more effectively. Partner church projects have always been central to how Crown Jesus Ministries operate, firmly believing that effective evangelism always works best within the context of a local church. By working with churches, the results are lasting, discipleship is effective and the local church is left better equipped to reach out and share the love of Jesus in their area.

If you would like Mitch or any of the team to visit your church or community, contact the Crown Jesus Ministries office on (028) 9073 8338 or email info@crownjesus.org

For more information, visit www.crownjesus.org

discover more great Christian books
at www.ivpbooks.com

Full details of all the books from Inter-Varsity Press – including
reader reviews, author information, videos and free downloads –
are available on our website at **www.ivpbooks.com**.

IVP publishes a wide range of books on various subjects including:

Biography

Christian Living

Bible Studies

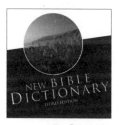
Reference

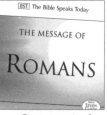
Commentaries

Theology

On the website you can also sign up for regular email newsletters,
tell others what you think about books you have read by posting
reviews, and locate your nearest Christian bookshop using the
Find a Store feature.

IVP publishes Christian books that are **true to the Bible**
and that **communicate the gospel, develop discipleship**
and **strengthen the church** for its mission in the world.